LEARNING TO FLY

by Chris Giarrusso

G-MAN™

LEARNING TO FLY

created, written & illustrated by

CHRIS GIARRUSSO

chrisGcomics.com

THE MIGHTY
SKULLBOY ARMY
appearances co-written
& co-illustrated by
JACOB CHABOT
beetlebugcomics.com

special thanks to
DAVE GIARRUSSO

IMAGE COMICS, INC.

Robert Kirkman - Chief Operating Officer
Erik Larsen - Chief Financial Officer
Todd McFarlane - President
Marc Silvestri - Chief Executive Officer
Jim Valentino - Vice-President

ericstephenson - Publisher
Joe Keatinge - PR & Marketing Coordinator
Branwyn Bigglestone - Accounts Manager
Tyler Shainline - Administrative Assistant
Traci Hui - Traffic Manager
Allen Hui - Production Manager
Drew Gill - Production Artist
Jonathan Chan - Production Artist
Monica Howard - Production Artist

www.imagecomics.com

ISBN: 978-1-60706-087-1

International Rights Representative:
Christine Jensen christine@gfloystudio.com

LEARNING TO FLY

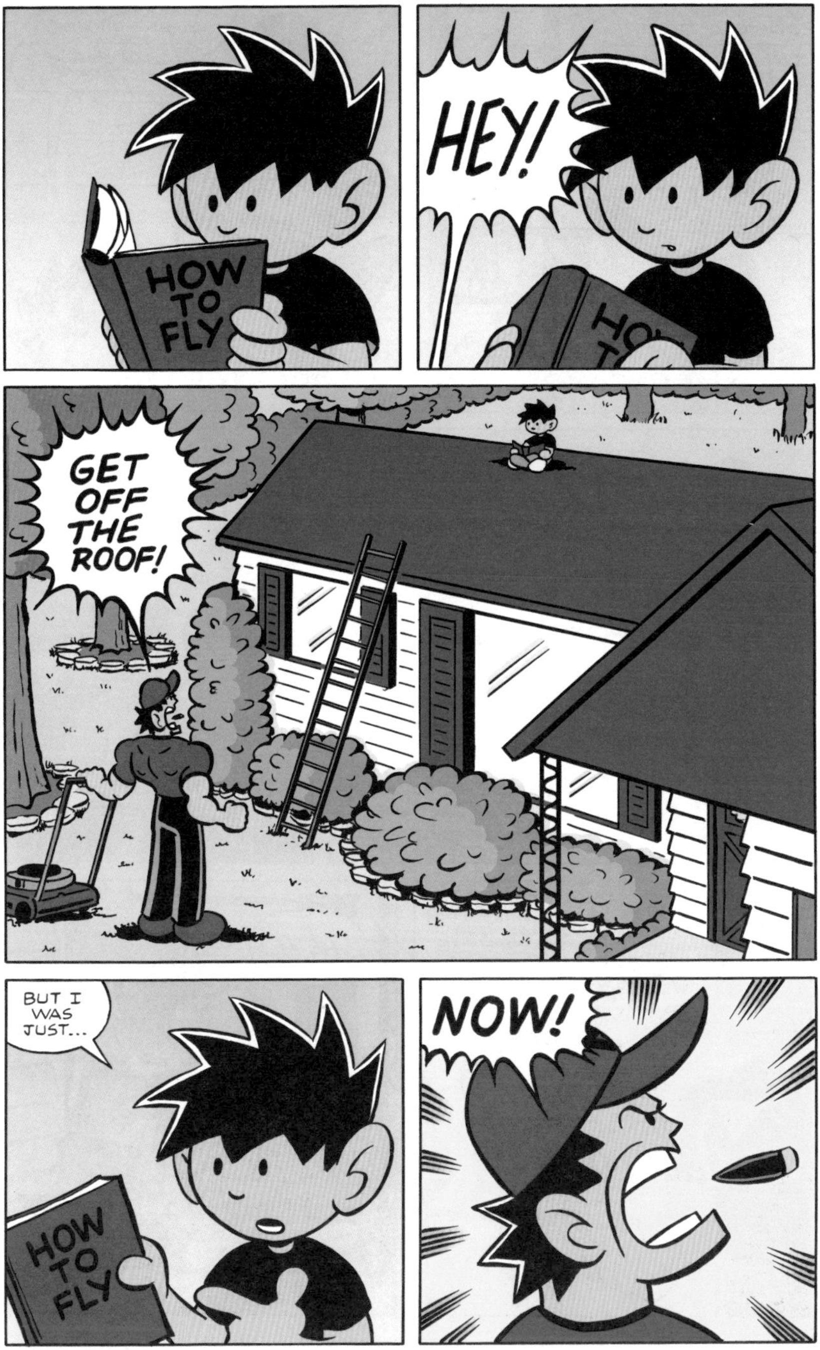
HOW TO FLY
HEY!
GET OFF THE ROOF!
BUT I WAS JUST...
HOW TO FLY
NOW!

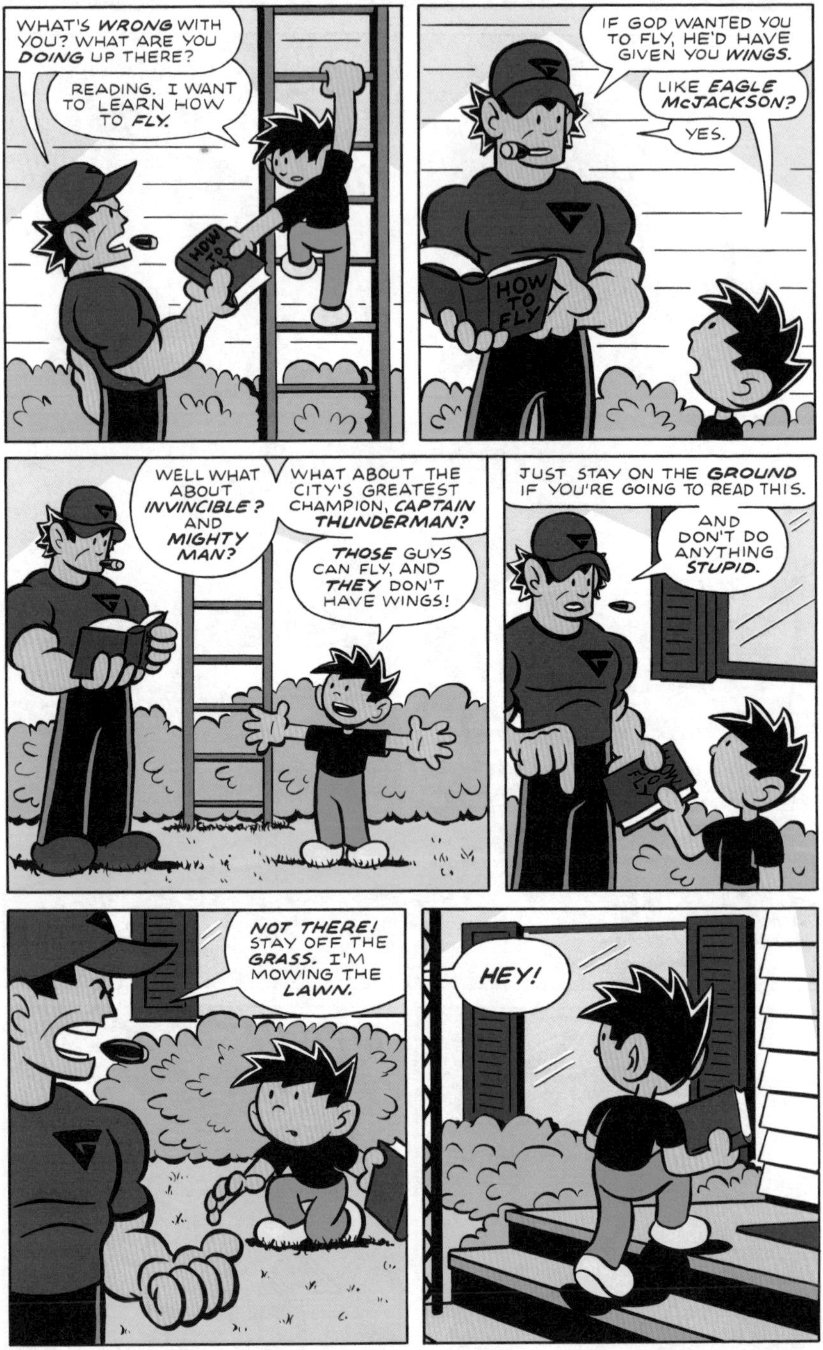
WHAT'S WRONG WITH YOU? WHAT ARE YOU DOING UP THERE?
READING. I WANT TO LEARN HOW TO FLY.
HOW TO FLY
IF GOD WANTED YOU TO FLY, HE'D HAVE GIVEN YOU WINGS.
LIKE EAGLE McJACKSON?
YES.
WELL WHAT ABOUT INVINCIBLE? AND MIGHTY MAN?
WHAT ABOUT THE CITY'S GREATEST CHAMPION, CAPTAIN THUNDERMAN?
THOSE GUYS CAN FLY, AND THEY DON'T HAVE WINGS!
JUST STAY ON THE GROUND IF YOU'RE GOING TO READ THIS.
AND DON'T DO ANYTHING STUPID.
NOT THERE! STAY OFF THE GRASS. I'M MOWING THE LAWN.
HEY!

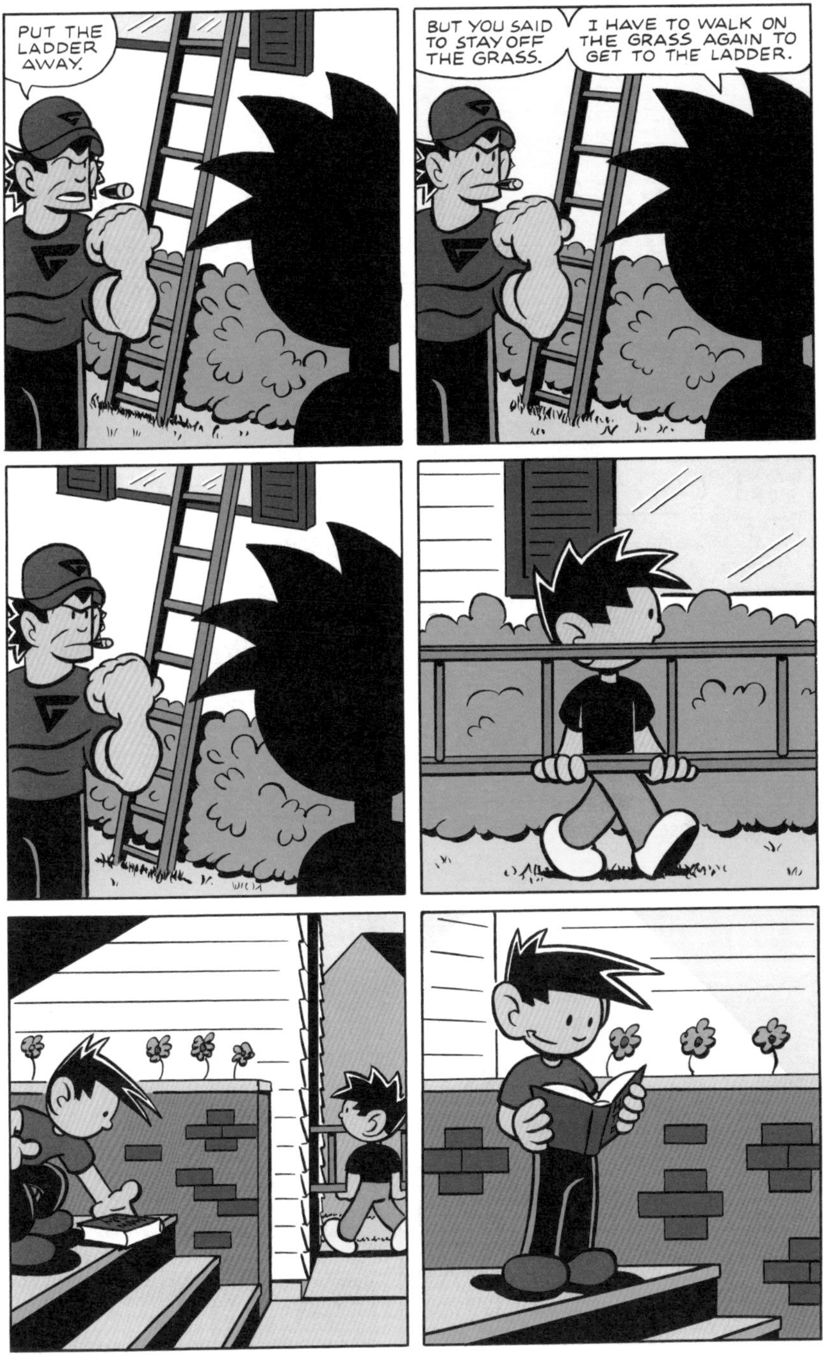
PUT THE LADDER AWAY.
BUT YOU SAID TO STAY OFF THE GRASS.
I HAVE TO WALK ON THE GRASS AGAIN TO GET TO THE LADDER.

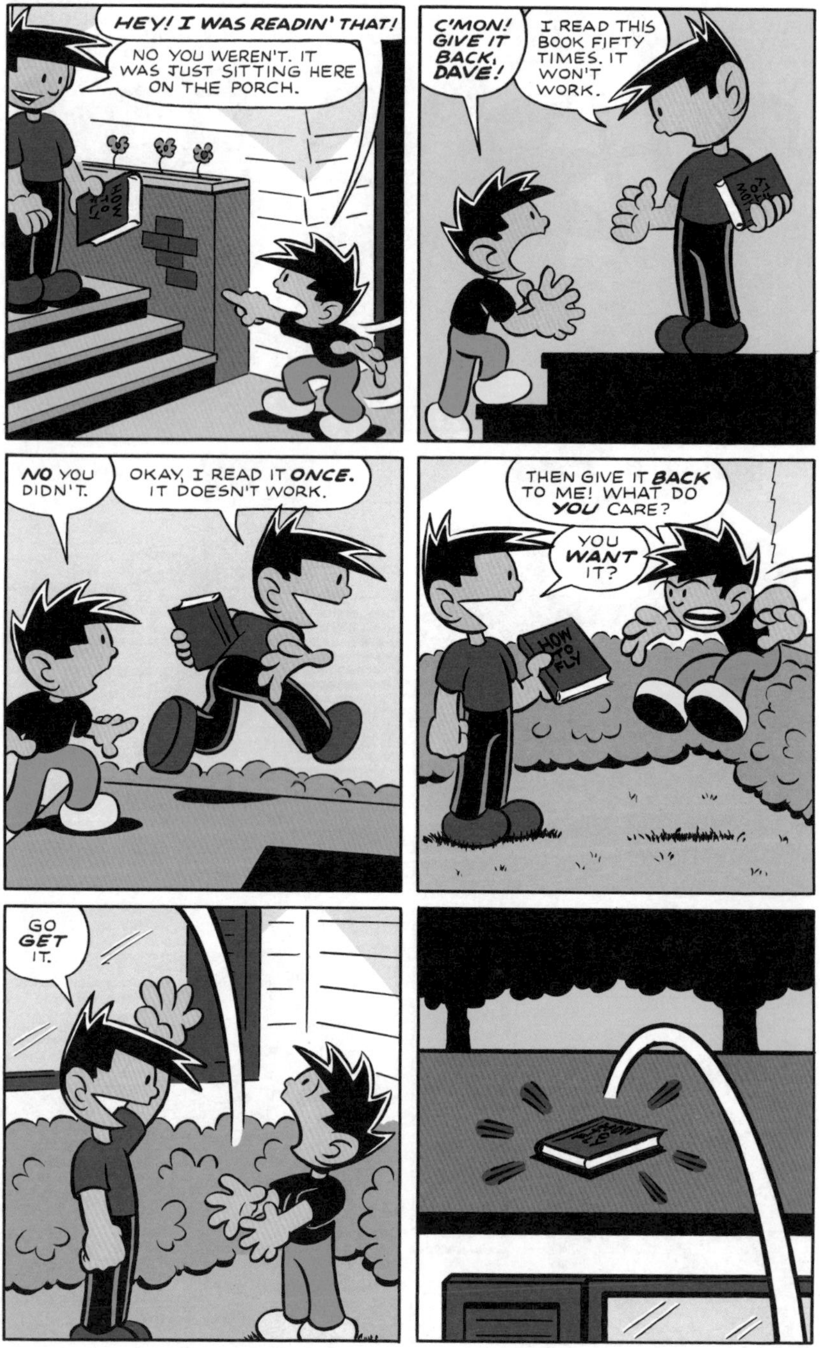
HEY! I WAS READIN' THAT!
NO YOU WEREN'T. IT WAS JUST SITTING HERE ON THE PORCH.
HOW TO FLY
C'MON! GIVE IT BACK, DAVE!
I READ THIS BOOK FIFTY TIMES. IT WON'T WORK.
NO YOU DIDN'T.
OKAY, I READ IT ONCE. IT DOESN'T WORK.
THEN GIVE IT BACK TO ME! WHAT DO YOU CARE?
YOU WANT IT?
HOW TO FLY
GO GET IT.

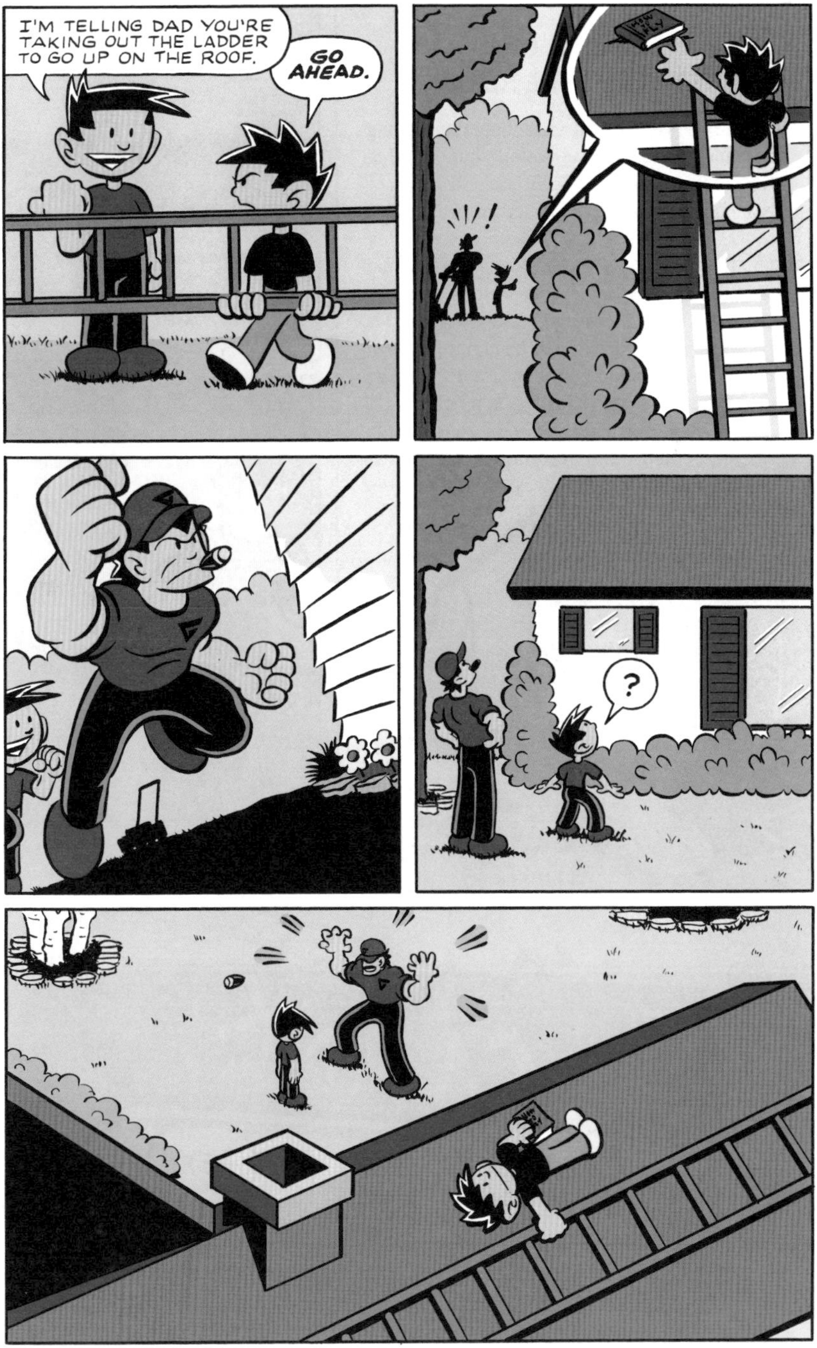
I'M TELLING DAD YOU'RE TAKING OUT THE LADDER TO GO UP ON THE ROOF.
GO AHEAD.
?

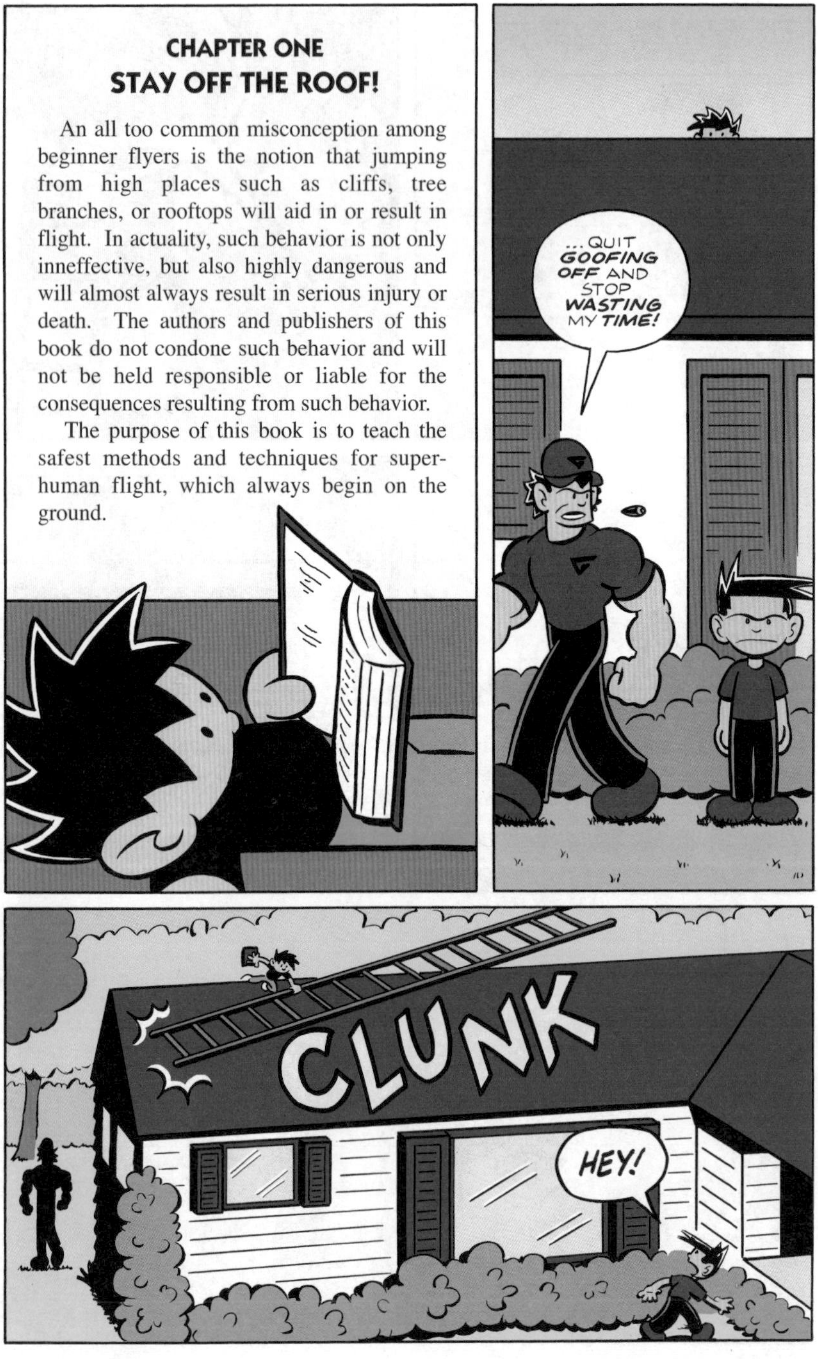
CHAPTER ONE
STAY OFF THE ROOF!
An all too common misconception among beginner flyers is the notion that jumping from high places such as cliffs, tree branches, or rooftops will aid in or result in flight. In actuality, such behavior is not only inneffective, but also highly dangerous and will almost always result in serious injury or death. The authors and publishers of this book do not condone such behavior and will not be held responsible or liable for the consequences resulting from such behavior.
The purpose of this book is to teach the safest methods and techniques for super-human flight, which always begin on the ground.
...QUIT GOOFING OFF AND STOP WASTING MY TIME!
CLUNK
HEY!

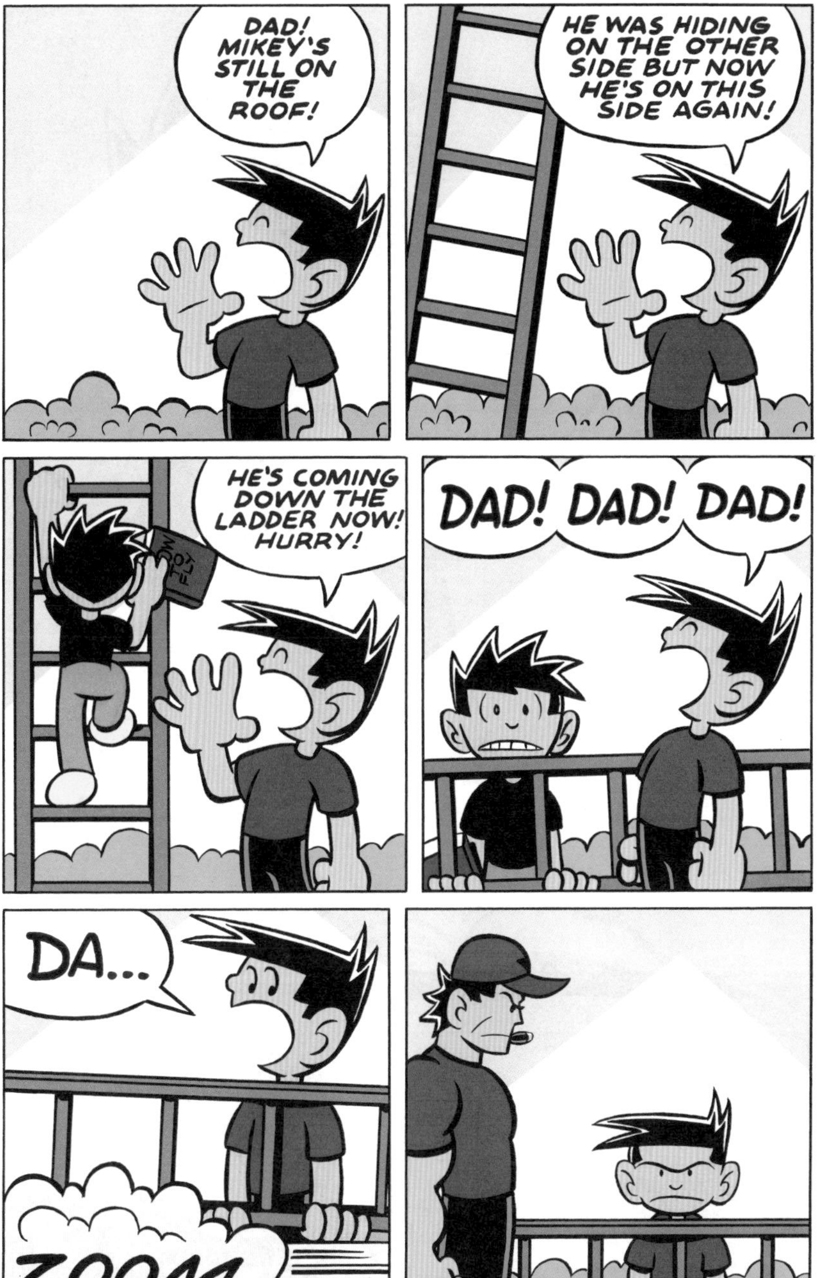
DAD! MIKEY'S STILL ON THE ROOF!
HE WAS HIDING ON THE OTHER SIDE BUT NOW HE'S ON THIS SIDE AGAIN!
HE'S COMING DOWN THE LADDER NOW! HURRY!
DAD! DAD! DAD!
DA...
ZOOM

CHAPTER THREE
LEVITATION

Levitation, or floating, is the first step towards achieving flight. If you are warmed up, in your proper attire, and on solid ground, you are ready to levitate.

To begin, get in your levitation stance and concentrate on supernaturally overcoming the forces of gravity. It is important to resist jumping, as jumping involves a state of mind that acknowledges the laws of physics -- the very laws we seek to ignore!

Through meditation, simply open a dialogue between the cells of your body and the molecules of the surrounding air, and you'll be levitating in no time!

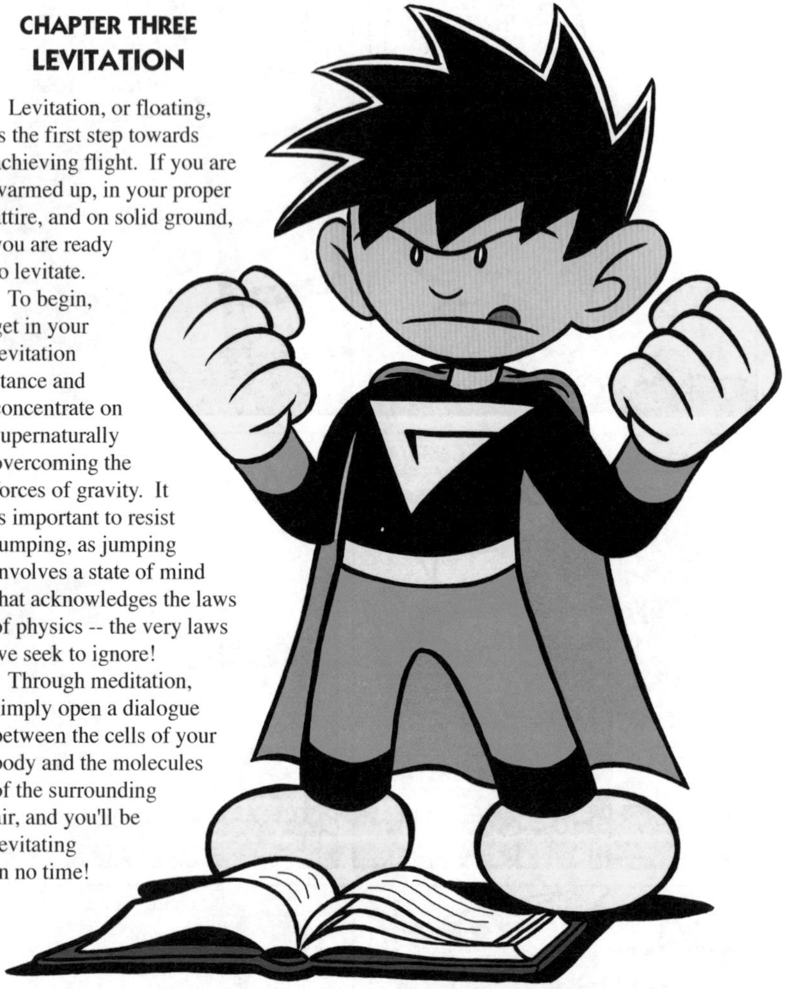

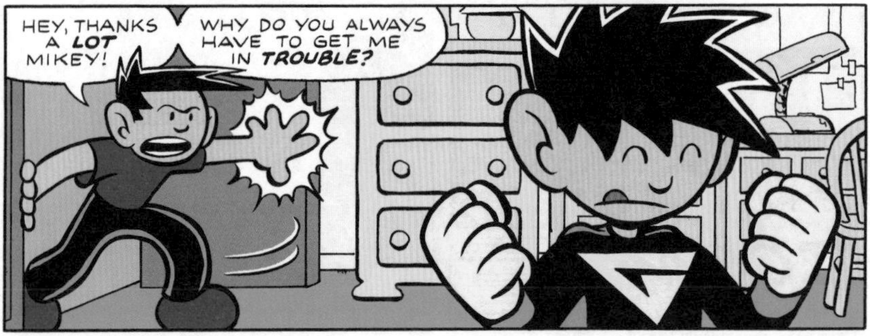
HEY, THANKS A LOT MIKEY!
WHY DO YOU ALWAYS HAVE TO GET ME IN TROUBLE?

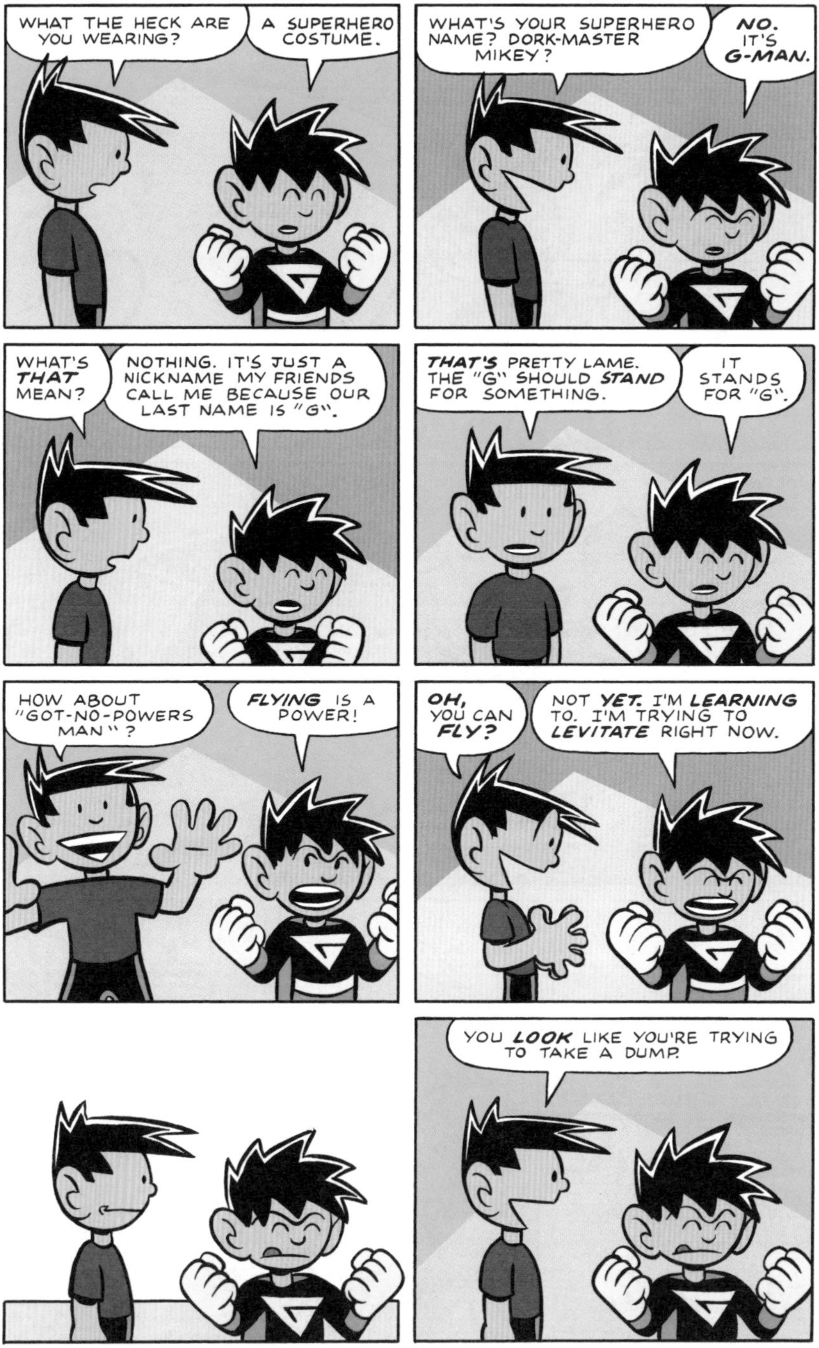
WHAT THE HECK ARE YOU WEARING?
A SUPERHERO COSTUME.
WHAT'S YOUR SUPERHERO NAME? DORK-MASTER MIKEY?
NO. IT'S G-MAN.
WHAT'S THAT MEAN?
NOTHING. IT'S JUST A NICKNAME MY FRIENDS CALL ME BECAUSE OUR LAST NAME IS "G".
THAT'S PRETTY LAME. THE "G" SHOULD STAND FOR SOMETHING.
IT STANDS FOR "G".
HOW ABOUT "GOT-NO-POWERS MAN"?
FLYING IS A POWER!
OH, YOU CAN FLY?
NOT YET. I'M LEARNING TO. I'M TRYING TO LEVITATE RIGHT NOW.
YOU LOOK LIKE YOU'RE TRYING TO TAKE A DUMP.

YOU SHOULD GET RID OF THIS CAPE. IT LOOKS STUPID.

LET GO! THE CAPE'S THE MOST IMPORTANT PART!

SEE?! IT SAYS SO RIGHT HERE!

The cape* is considered by many to be the most important part of the flight uniform because wearing a cape helps to convince your environment that gravity holds no power over you.

Wind re... is not a f... in flight, ... are most... laws of ... scienc...

YEAH, WHATEVER. I ALREADY READ THAT BOOK.

I TOLD YOU IT DOESN'T WORK.

WHAT THE--?

MISSED THAT PART BEFORE!

...conside... to be the... part of th... because w... helps to con... environm... gravity ho... no power over you.

*Magic capes work best.

...LAST NIGHT WHEN CAPTAIN THUNDERMAN ENDED MISTER MENTAL'S CRIMINAL RAMPAGE BY TOSSING HIM INTO THE CITY VOLCANO. IN OTHER NEWS...

HEY MOM, WHERE'S OUR MAGIC BLANKET?

CHECK THE HALL CLOSET.

SNIP SNIP

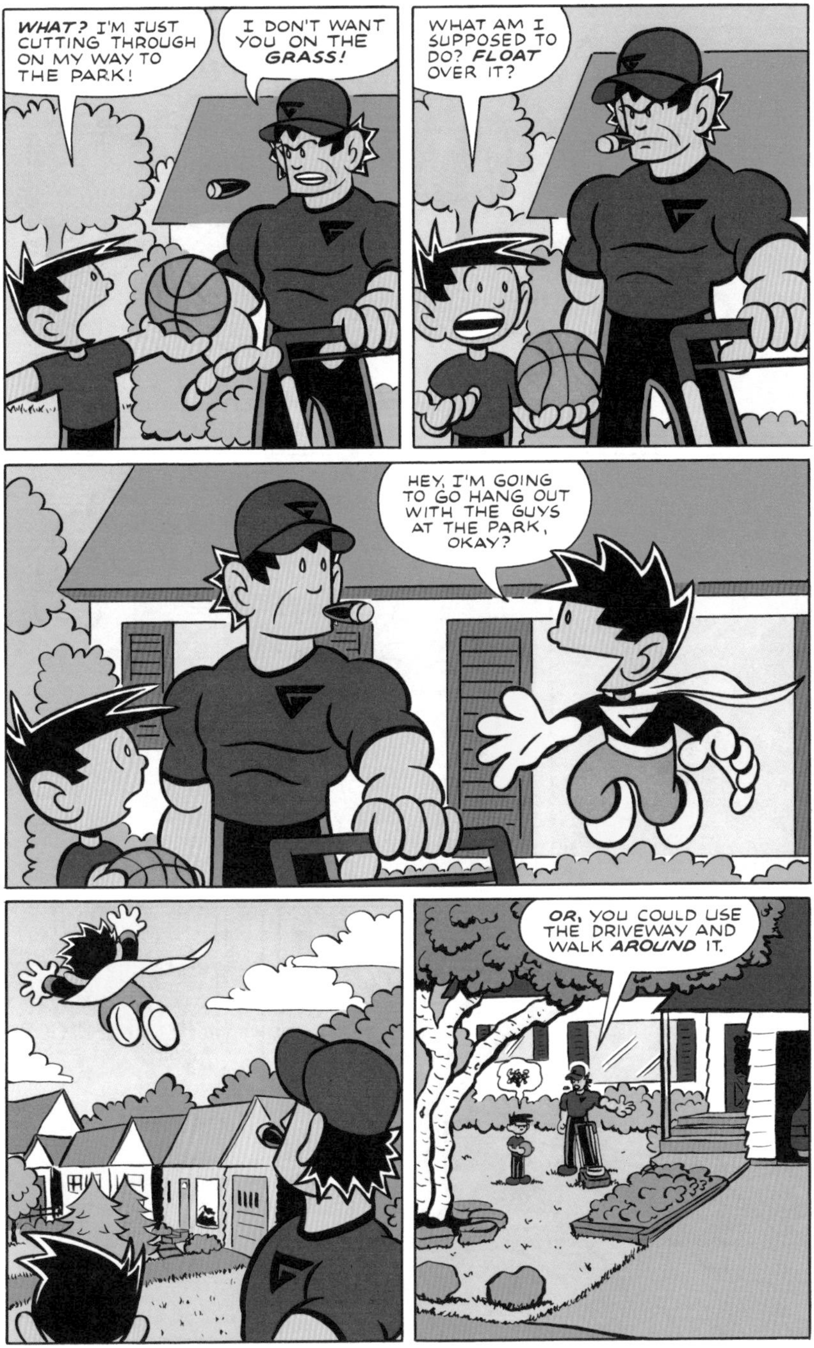
WHAT? I'M JUST CUTTING THROUGH ON MY WAY TO THE PARK!
I DON'T WANT YOU ON THE GRASS!
WHAT AM I SUPPOSED TO DO? FLOAT OVER IT?
HEY, I'M GOING TO GO HANG OUT WITH THE GUYS AT THE PARK, OKAY?
OR, YOU COULD USE THE DRIVEWAY AND WALK AROUND IT.

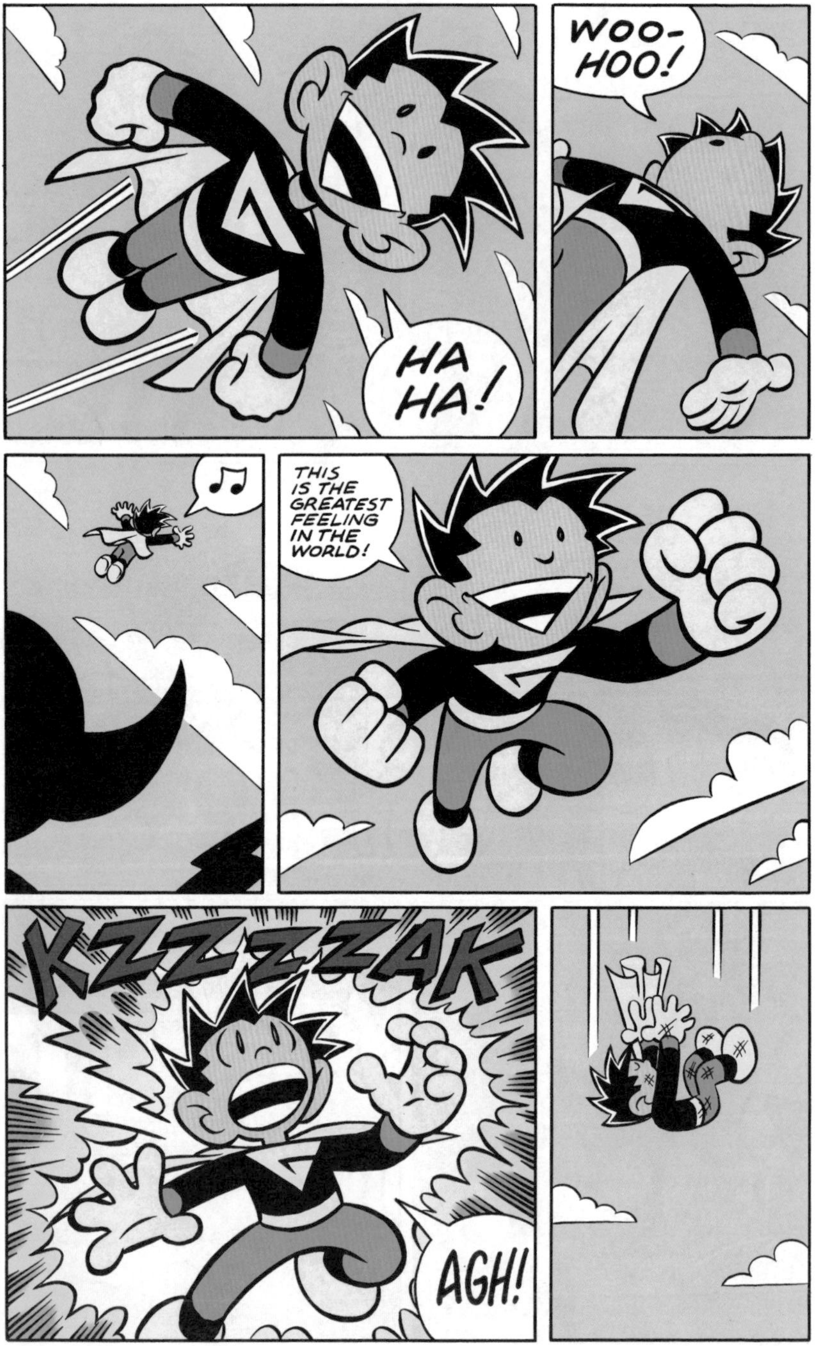
HA HA!
WOO-HOO!
♫
THIS IS THE GREATEST FEELING IN THE WORLD!
KZZZZZAK
AGH!

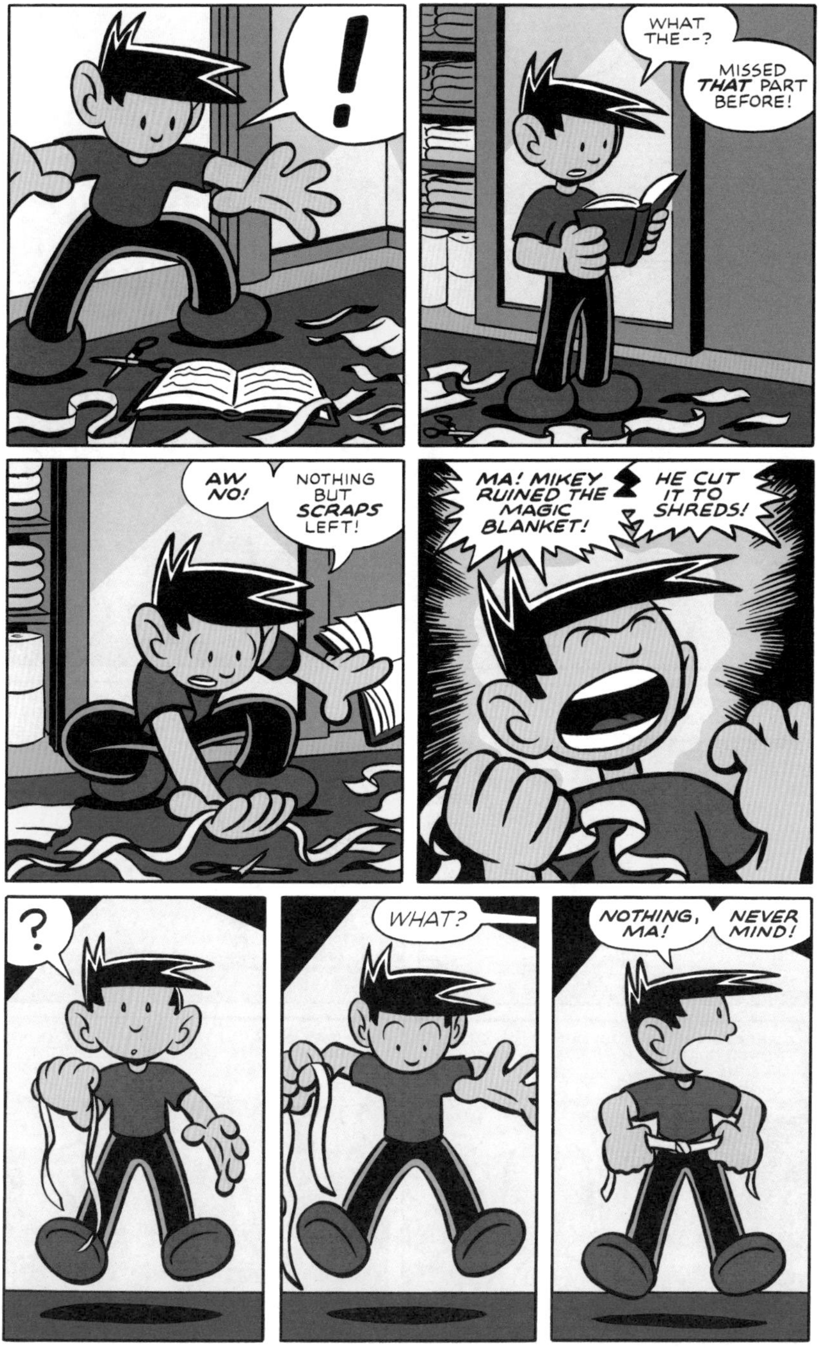
!
WHAT THE--?
MISSED THAT PART BEFORE!
AW NO!
NOTHING BUT SCRAPS LEFT!
MA! MIKEY RUINED THE MAGIC BLANKET!
HE CUT IT TO SHREDS!
?
WHAT?
NOTHING, MA!
NEVER MIND!

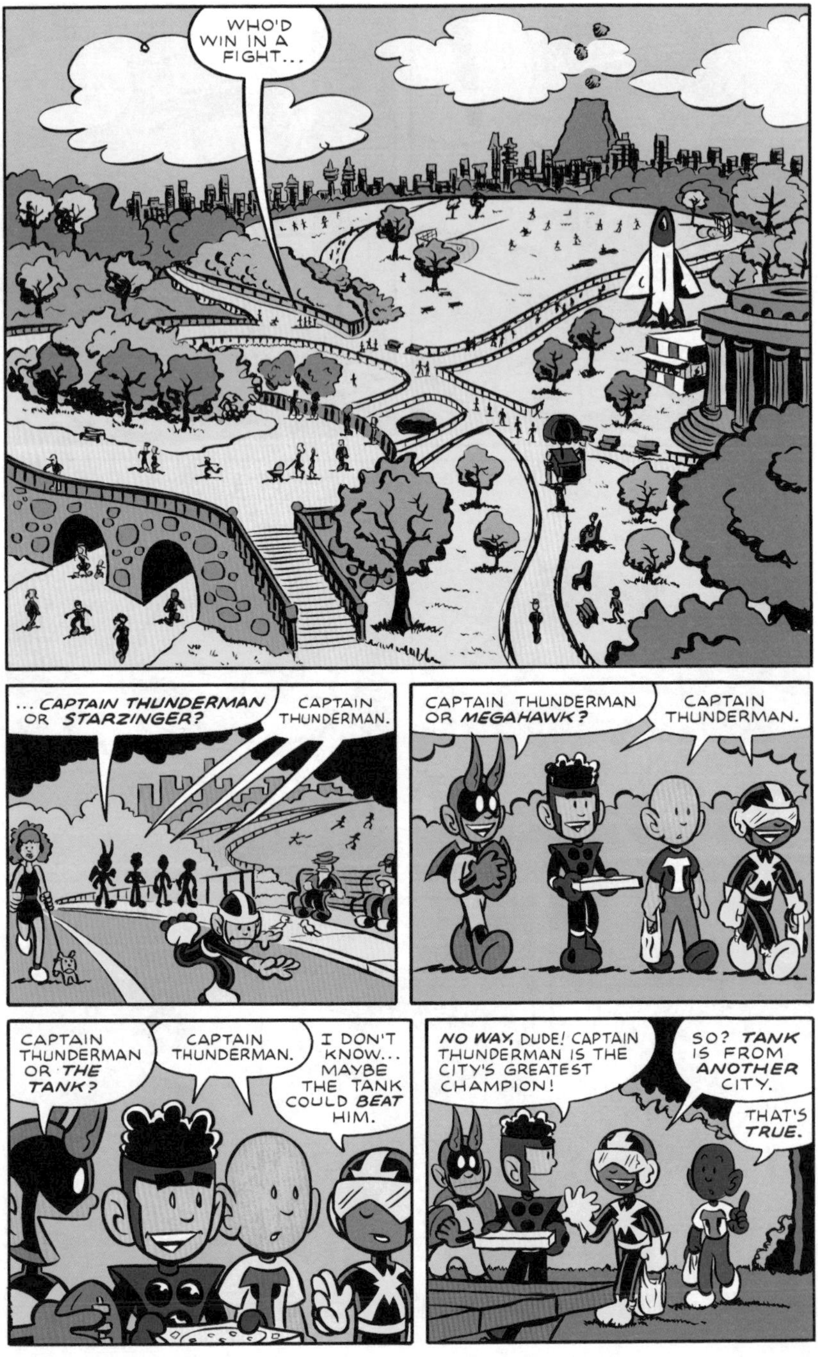
WHO'D WIN IN A FIGHT...
...CAPTAIN THUNDERMAN OR STARZINGER?
CAPTAIN THUNDERMAN.
CAPTAIN THUNDERMAN OR MEGAHAWK?
CAPTAIN THUNDERMAN.
CAPTAIN THUNDERMAN OR THE TANK?
CAPTAIN THUNDERMAN.
I DON'T KNOW... MAYBE THE TANK COULD BEAT HIM.
NO WAY, DUDE! CAPTAIN THUNDERMAN IS THE CITY'S GREATEST CHAMPION!
SO? TANK IS FROM ANOTHER CITY.
THAT'S TRUE.

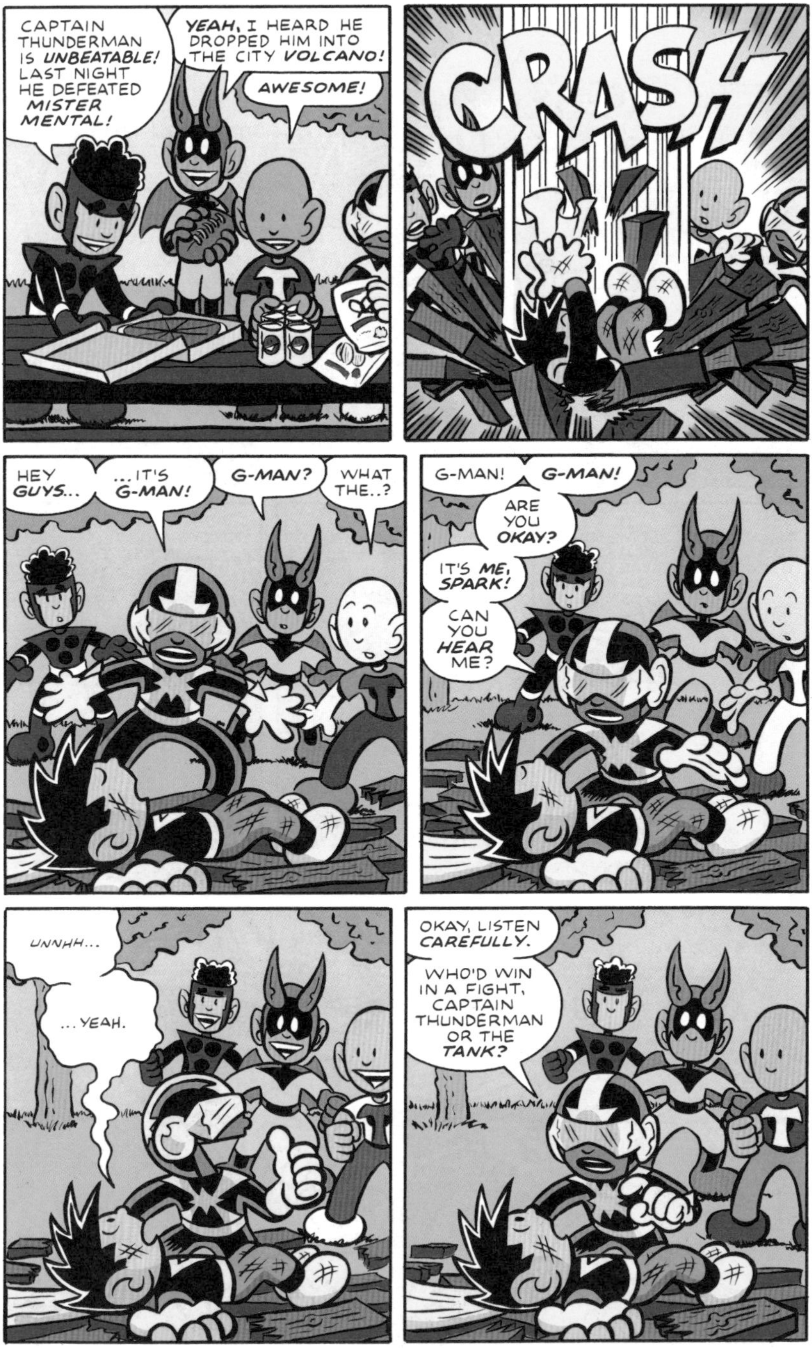
CAPTAIN THUNDERMAN IS UNBEATABLE! LAST NIGHT HE DEFEATED MISTER MENTAL!
YEAH, I HEARD HE DROPPED HIM INTO THE CITY VOLCANO!
AWESOME!
CRASH
HEY GUYS...
...IT'S G-MAN!
G-MAN?
WHAT THE..?
G-MAN!
G-MAN!
ARE YOU OKAY?
IT'S ME, SPARK!
CAN YOU HEAR ME?
UNNHH...
...YEAH.
OKAY, LISTEN CAREFULLY.
WHO'D WIN IN A FIGHT, CAPTAIN THUNDERMAN OR THE TANK?

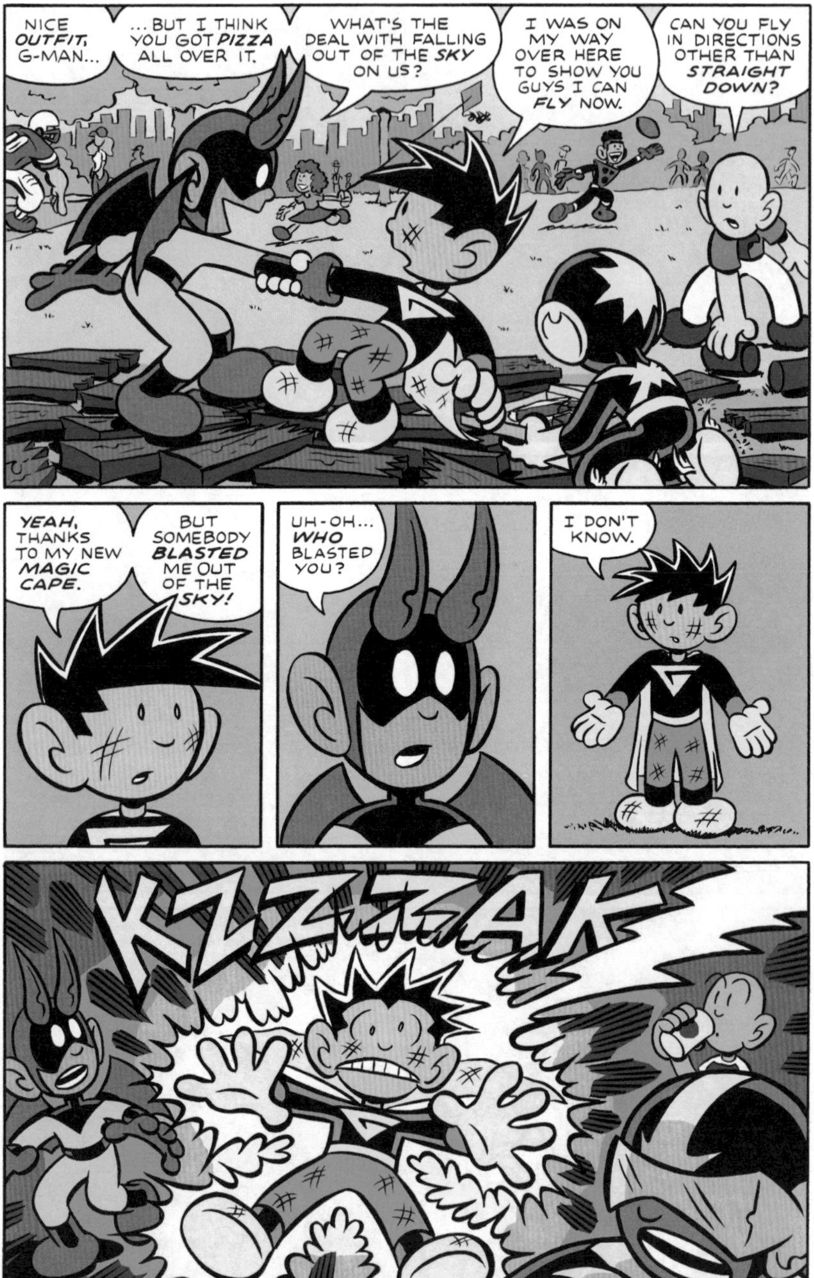
NICE OUTFIT, G-MAN...
...BUT I THINK YOU GOT PIZZA ALL OVER IT.
WHAT'S THE DEAL WITH FALLING OUT OF THE SKY ON US?
I WAS ON MY WAY OVER HERE TO SHOW YOU GUYS I CAN FLY NOW.
CAN YOU FLY IN DIRECTIONS OTHER THAN STRAIGHT DOWN?
YEAH, THANKS TO MY NEW MAGIC CAPE.
BUT SOMEBODY BLASTED ME OUT OF THE SKY!
UH-OH... WHO BLASTED YOU?
I DON'T KNOW.
KZZZAK

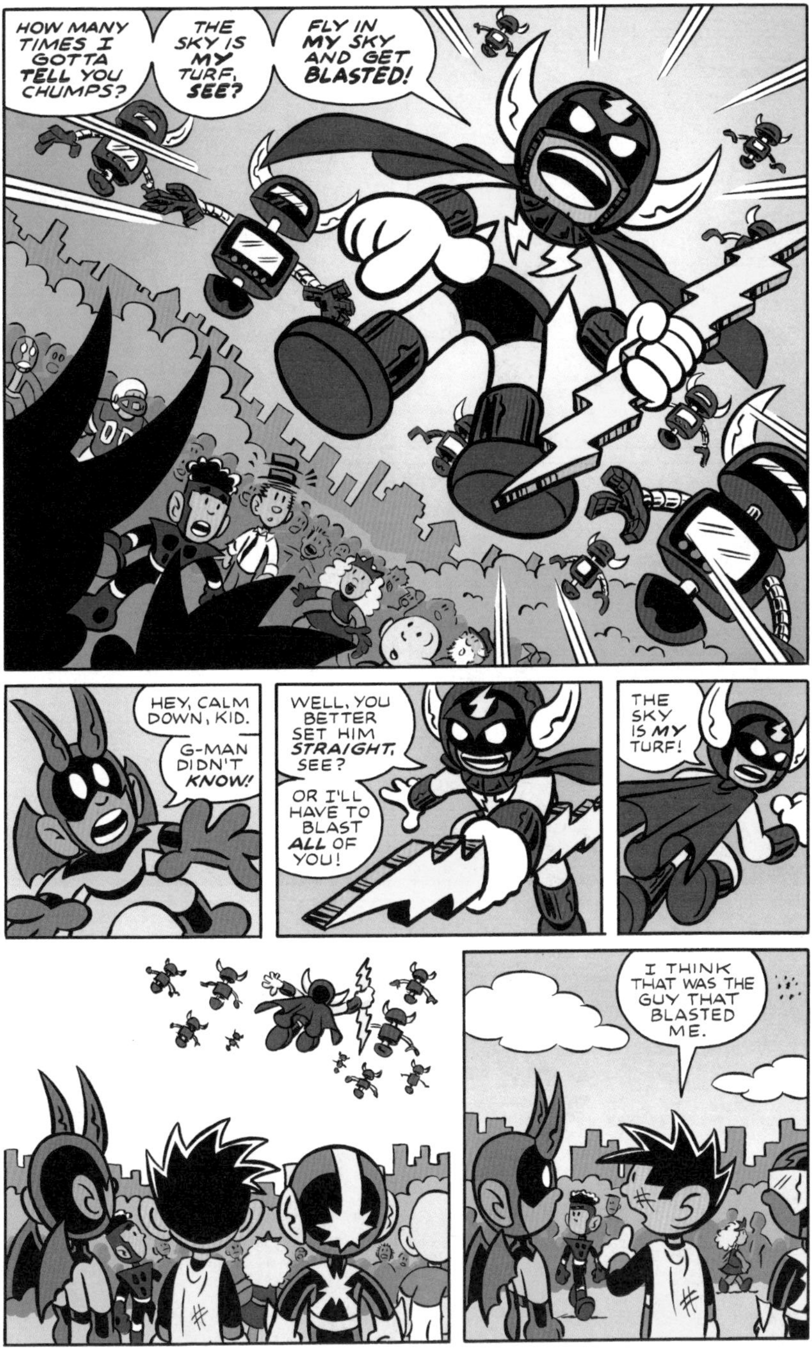
HOW MANY TIMES I GOTTA TELL YOU CHUMPS?
THE SKY IS MY TURF, SEE?
FLY IN MY SKY AND GET BLASTED!
HEY, CALM DOWN, KID.
G-MAN DIDN'T KNOW!
WELL, YOU BETTER SET HIM STRAIGHT, SEE?
OR I'LL HAVE TO BLAST ALL OF YOU!
THE SKY IS MY TURF!
I THINK THAT WAS THE GUY THAT BLASTED ME.

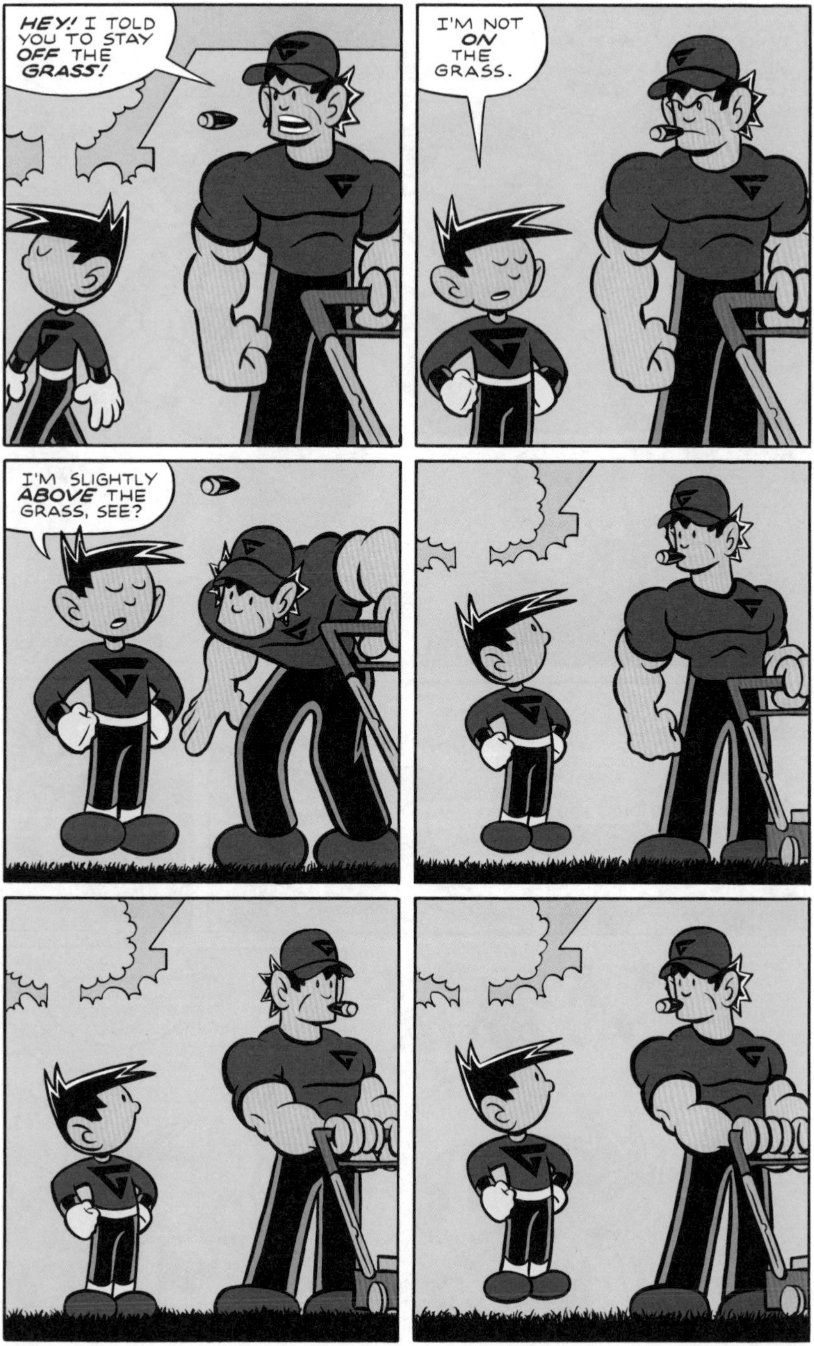
HEY! I TOLD YOU TO STAY OFF THE GRASS!
I'M NOT ON THE GRASS.
I'M SLIGHTLY ABOVE THE GRASS, SEE?

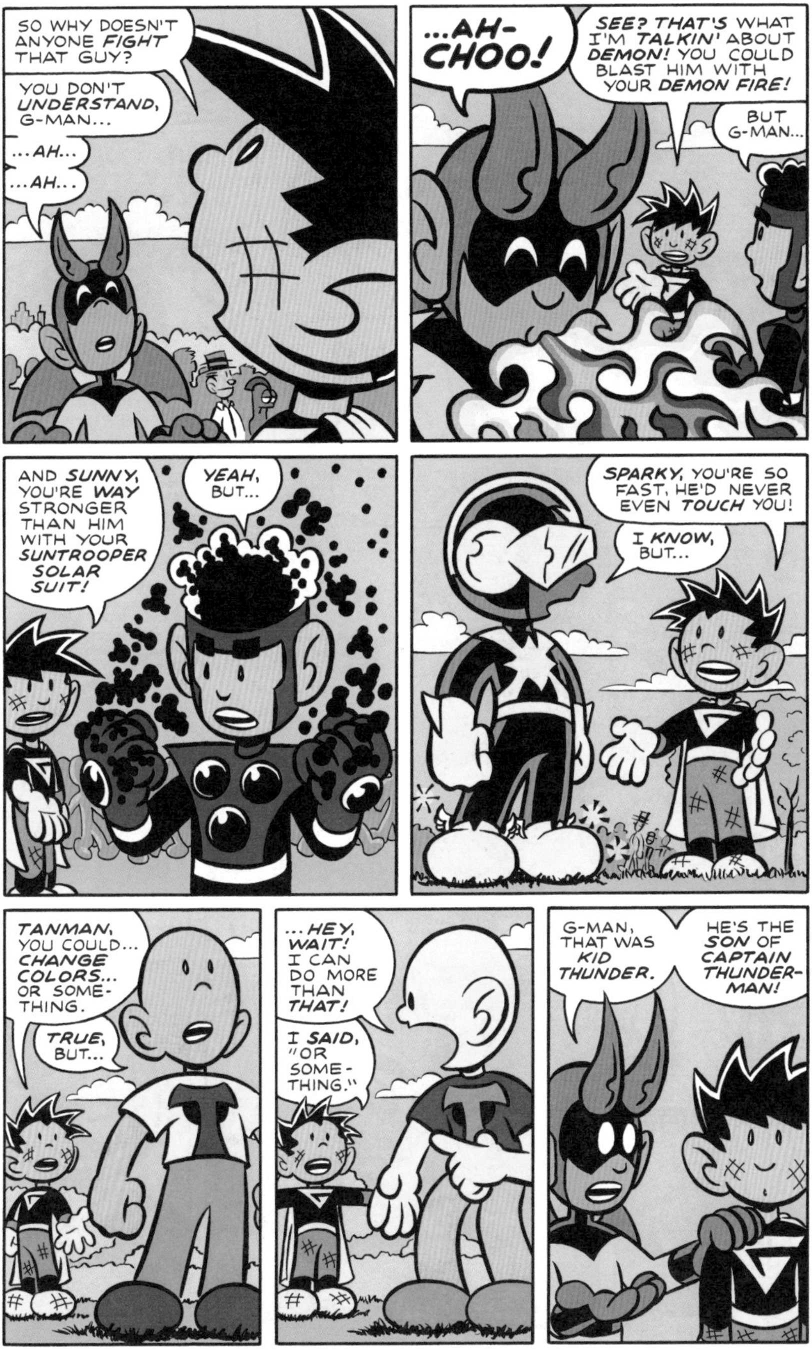
SO WHY DOESN'T ANYONE FIGHT THAT GUY?
YOU DON'T UNDERSTAND, G-MAN...
...AH...
...AH...
...AH-CHOO!
SEE? THAT'S WHAT I'M TALKIN' ABOUT DEMON! YOU COULD BLAST HIM WITH YOUR DEMON FIRE!
BUT G-MAN...
AND SUNNY, YOU'RE WAY STRONGER THAN HIM WITH YOUR SUNTROOPER SOLAR SUIT!
YEAH, BUT...
SPARKY, YOU'RE SO FAST, HE'D NEVER EVEN TOUCH YOU!
I KNOW, BUT...
TANMAN, YOU COULD... CHANGE COLORS... OR SOME-THING.
TRUE, BUT...
...HEY, WAIT! I CAN DO MORE THAN THAT!
I SAID, "OR SOME-THING."
G-MAN, THAT WAS KID THUNDER.
HE'S THE SON OF CAPTAIN THUNDER-MAN!

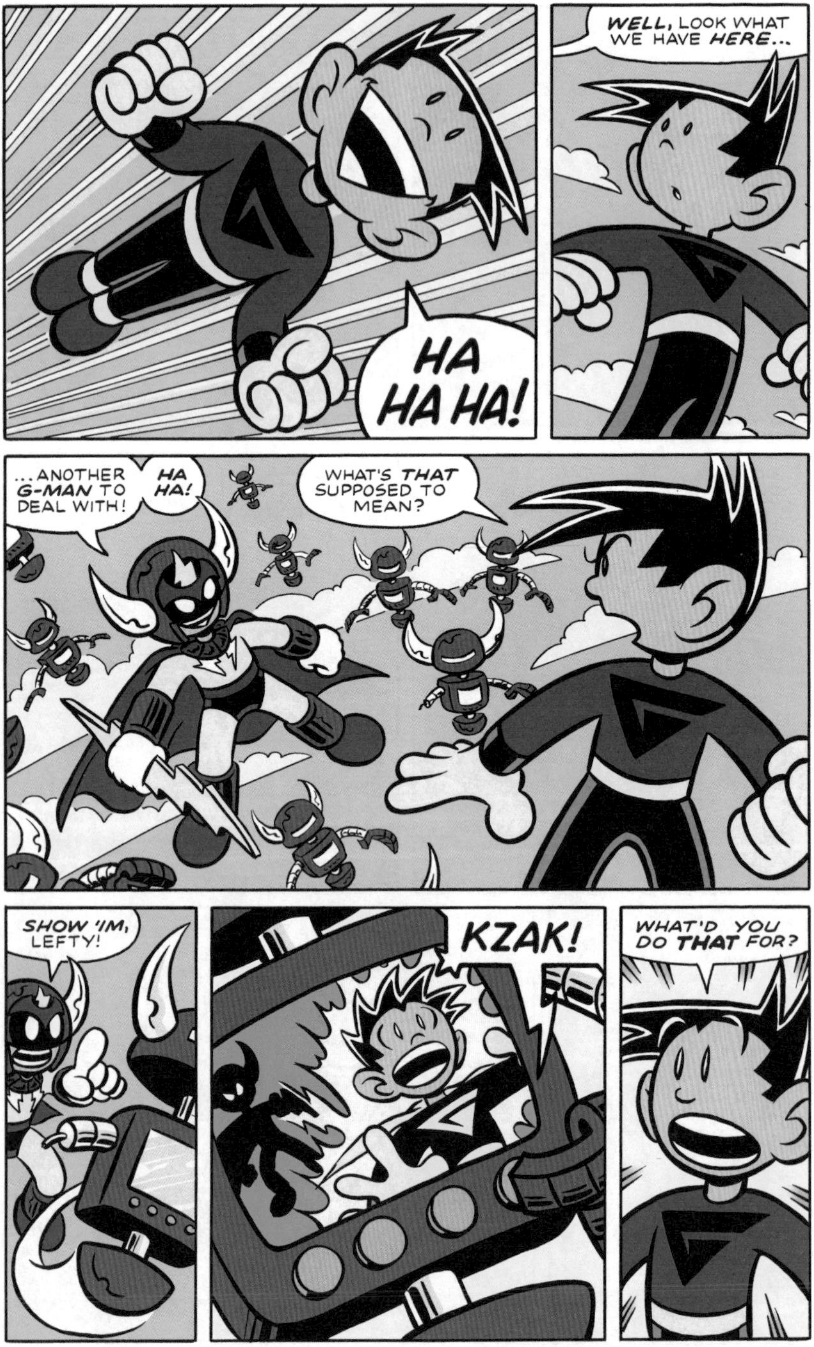
HA HA HA!
WELL, LOOK WHAT WE HAVE HERE...
...ANOTHER G-MAN TO DEAL WITH!
HA HA!
WHAT'S THAT SUPPOSED TO MEAN?
SHOW 'IM, LEFTY!
KZAK!
WHAT'D YOU DO THAT FOR?

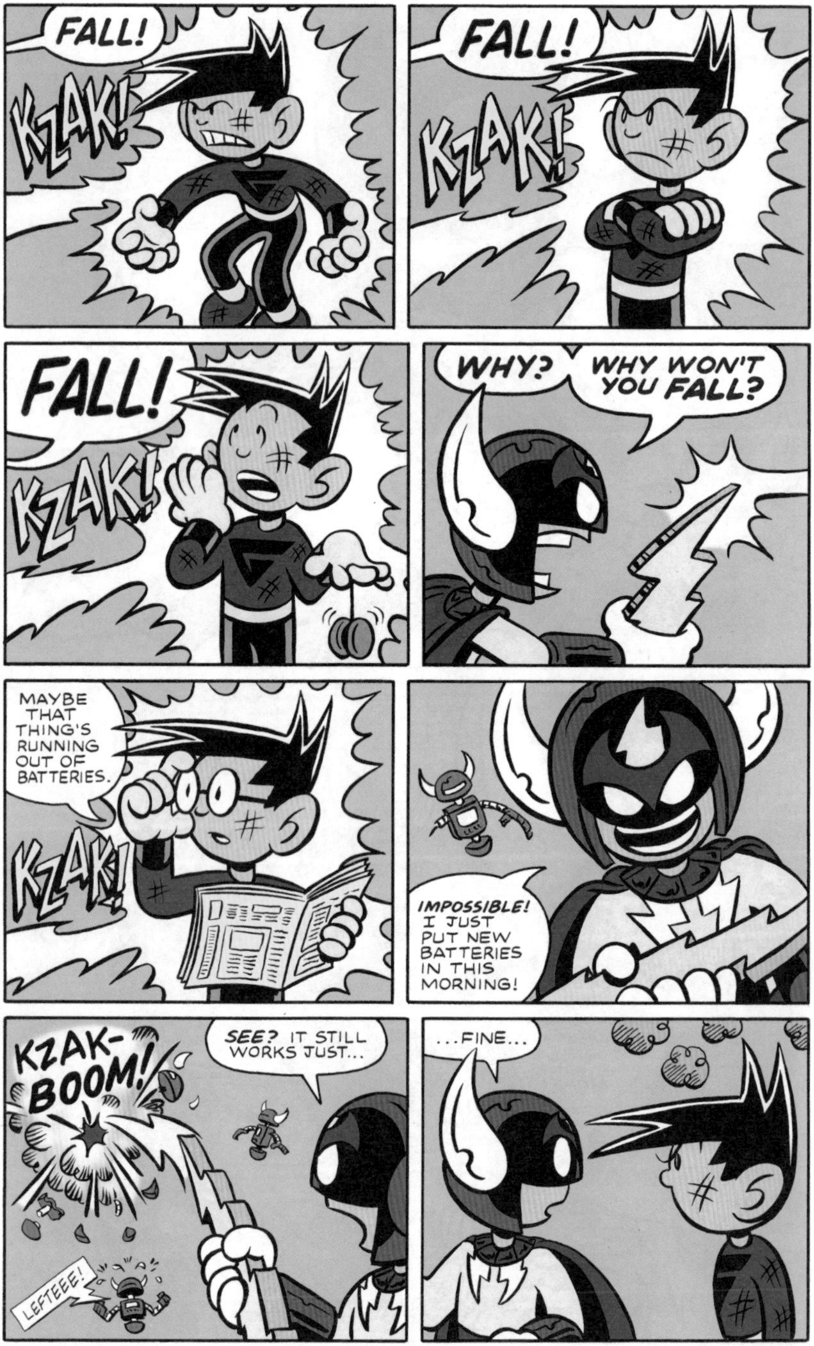
FALL!
KZAK!
FALL!
KZAK!
FALL!
KZAK!
WHY?
WHY WON'T YOU FALL?
MAYBE THAT THING'S RUNNING OUT OF BATTERIES.
KZAK!
IMPOSSIBLE! I JUST PUT NEW BATTERIES IN THIS MORNING!
KZAK-BOOM!
SEE? IT STILL WORKS JUST...
LEFTEEE!
...FINE...

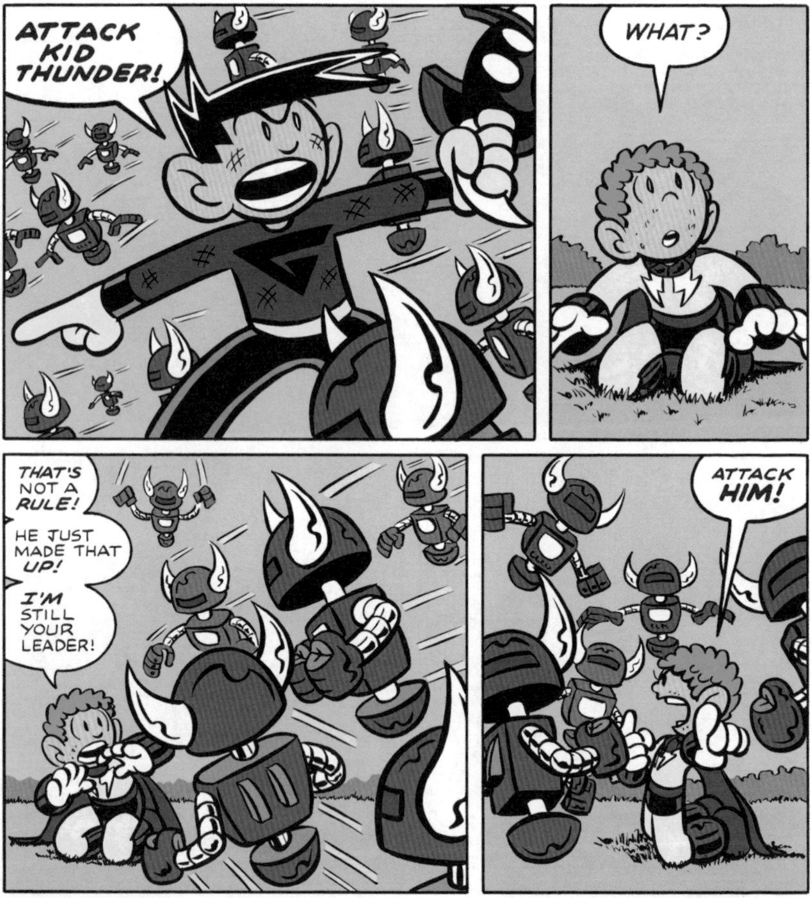
ATTACK KID THUNDER!
WHAT?
THAT'S NOT A RULE!
HE JUST MADE THAT UP!
I'M STILL YOUR LEADER!
ATTACK HIM!
LOOK, I'M WEARING THE HELMET OF LEADERSHIP!
OBEY ME!
THE HELMET MEANS NOTHING! I MADE YOU! OBEY ME!

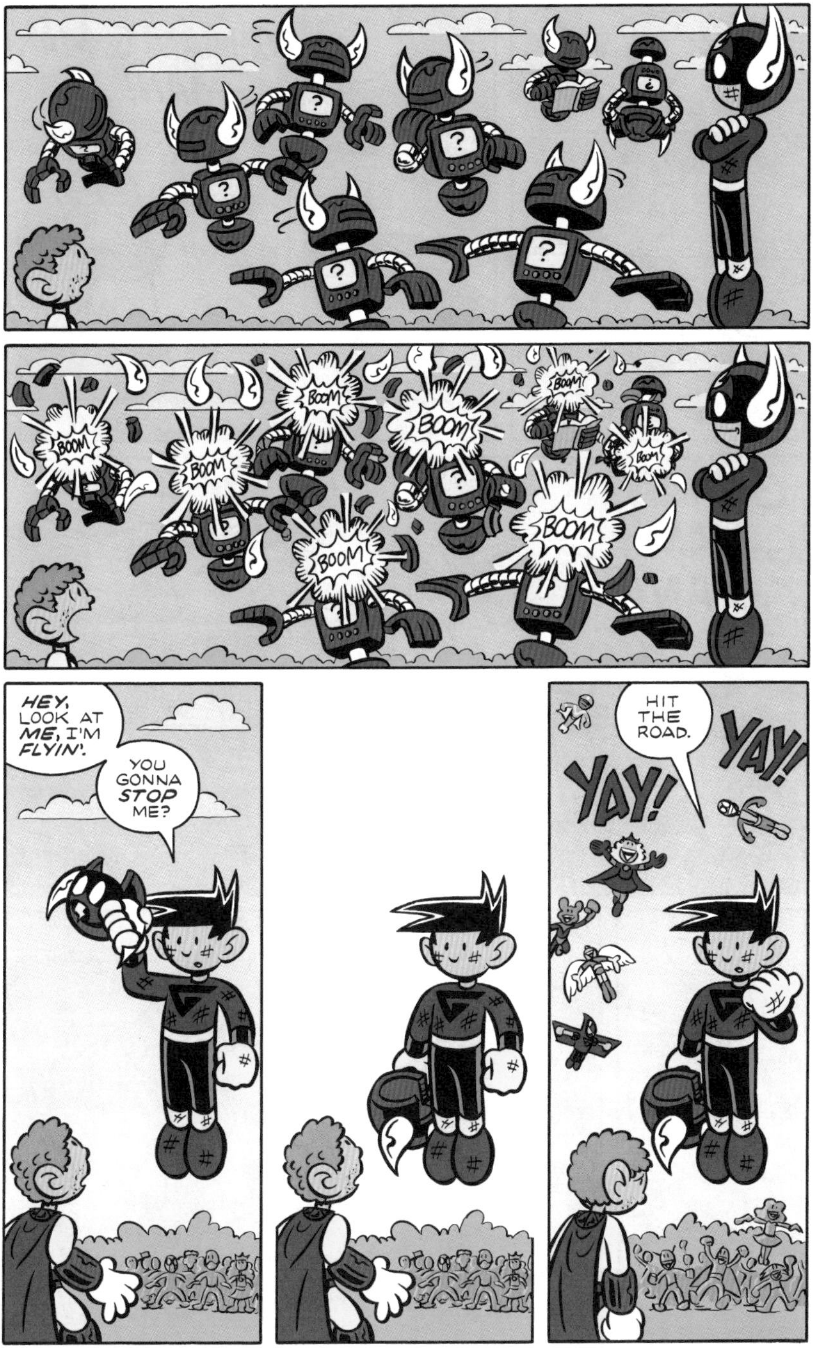
BOOM
BOOM
BOOM
BOOM
BOOM
BOOM
BOOM
BOOM
HEY, LOOK AT ME, I'M FLYIN'.
YOU GONNA STOP ME?
HIT THE ROAD.
YAY!
YAY!

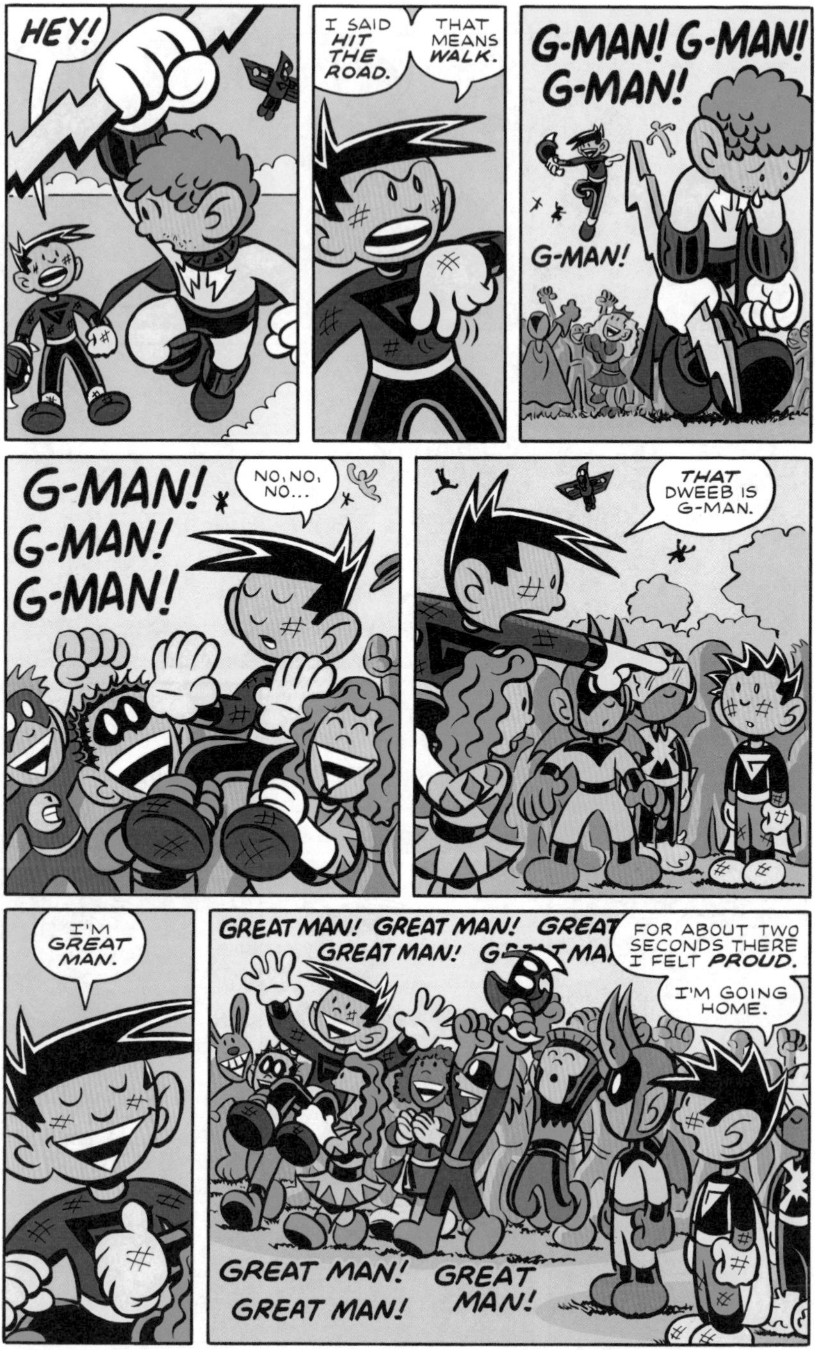
HEY!
I SAID HIT THE ROAD.
THAT MEANS WALK.
G-MAN! G-MAN! G-MAN!
G-MAN!
G-MAN! G-MAN! G-MAN!
NO, NO, NO...
THAT DWEEB IS G-MAN.
I'M GREAT MAN.
GREAT MAN! GREAT MAN! GREAT
GREAT MAN!
FOR ABOUT TWO SECONDS THERE I FELT PROUD.
I'M GOING HOME.
GREAT MAN! GREAT MAN!
GREAT MAN! GREAT MAN!

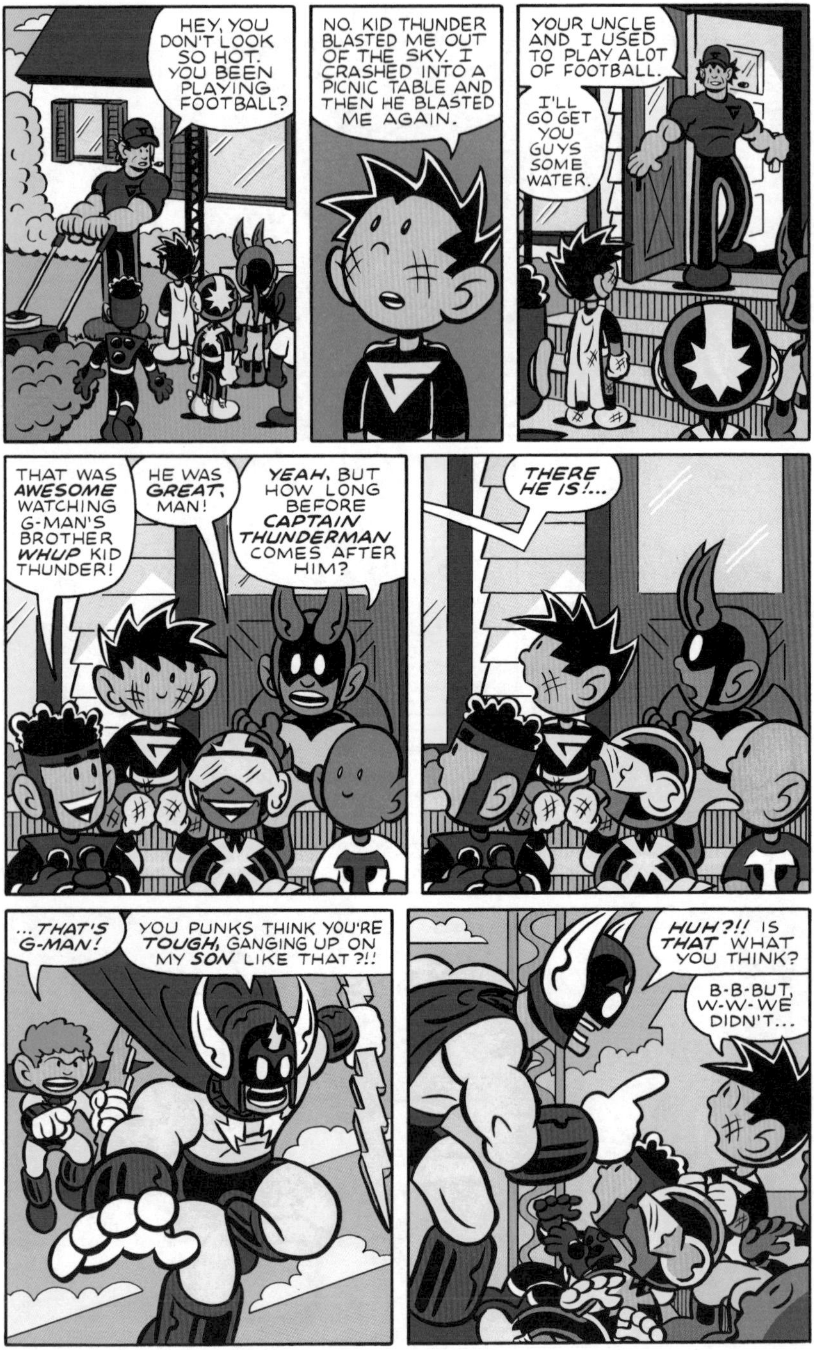
HEY, YOU DON'T LOOK SO HOT. YOU BEEN PLAYING FOOTBALL?
NO. KID THUNDER BLASTED ME OUT OF THE SKY. I CRASHED INTO A PICNIC TABLE AND THEN HE BLASTED ME AGAIN.
YOUR UNCLE AND I USED TO PLAY A LOT OF FOOTBALL.
I'LL GO GET YOU GUYS SOME WATER.
THAT WAS **AWESOME** WATCHING G-MAN'S BROTHER **WHUP** KID THUNDER!
HE WAS **GREAT,** MAN!
YEAH, BUT HOW LONG BEFORE **CAPTAIN THUNDERMAN** COMES AFTER HIM?
THERE HE IS!...
...THAT'S G-MAN!
YOU PUNKS THINK YOU'RE **TOUGH,** GANGING UP ON MY **SON** LIKE THAT?!!
HUH?!! IS **THAT** WHAT YOU THINK?
B-B-BUT, W-W-WE DIDN'T...

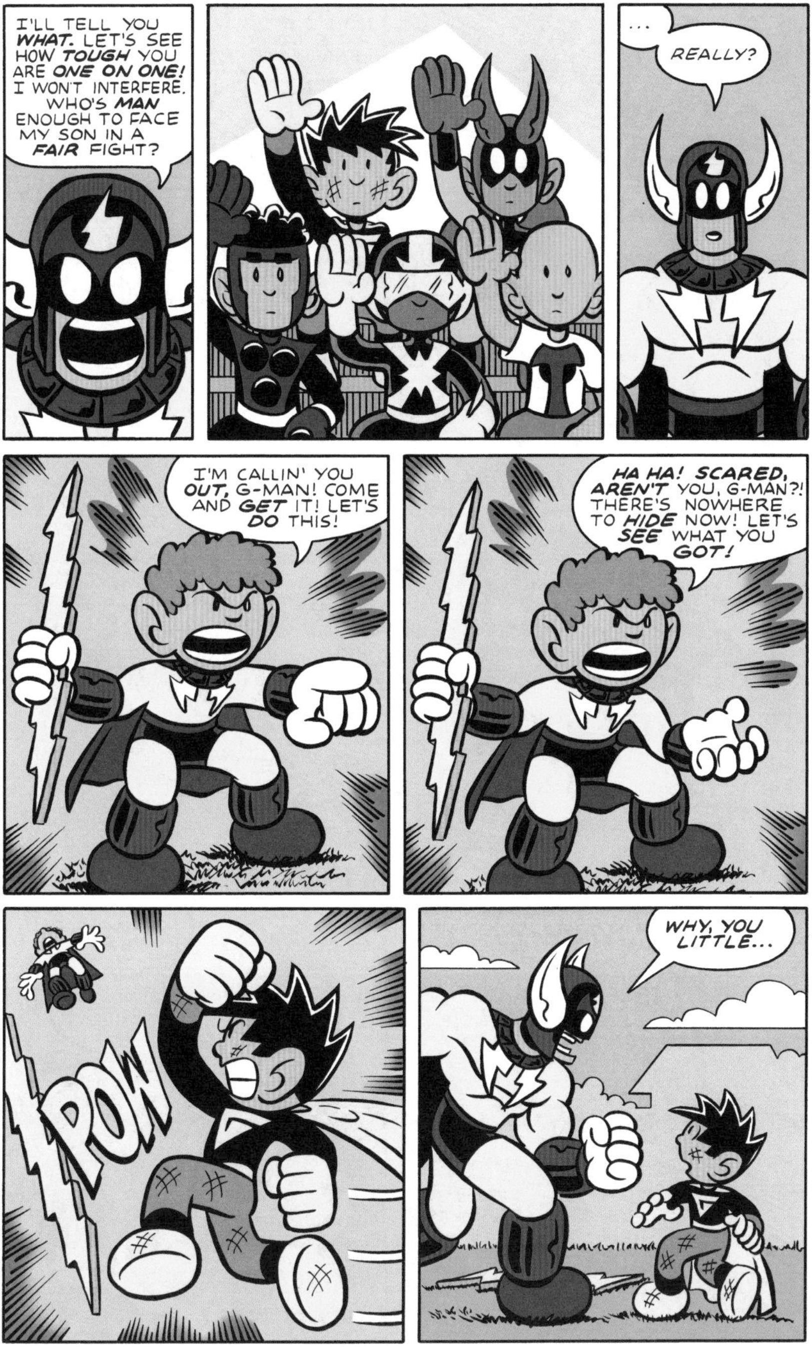
I'LL TELL YOU WHAT. LET'S SEE HOW TOUGH YOU ARE ONE ON ONE! I WON'T INTERFERE. WHO'S MAN ENOUGH TO FACE MY SON IN A FAIR FIGHT?
...
REALLY?
I'M CALLIN' YOU OUT, G-MAN! COME AND GET IT! LET'S DO THIS!
HA HA! SCARED, AREN'T YOU, G-MAN?! THERE'S NOWHERE TO HIDE NOW! LET'S SEE WHAT YOU GOT!
POW
WHY, YOU LITTLE...

BOOM!

YOU THINK *FIRE* AND *SOLAR ENERGY* CAN HURT ME? I'VE GOT *MOLTEN MAGMA* RUNNING THROUGH MY VEINS!

I GUESS YOU DON'T HAVE TO WORRY ABOUT *VAMPIRES* THEN, HUH?

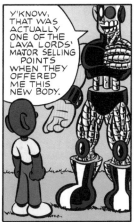

Y'KNOW, THAT WAS ACTUALLY ONE OF THE LAVA LORDS' MAJOR SELLING POINTS WHEN THEY OFFERED ME THIS NEW BODY.

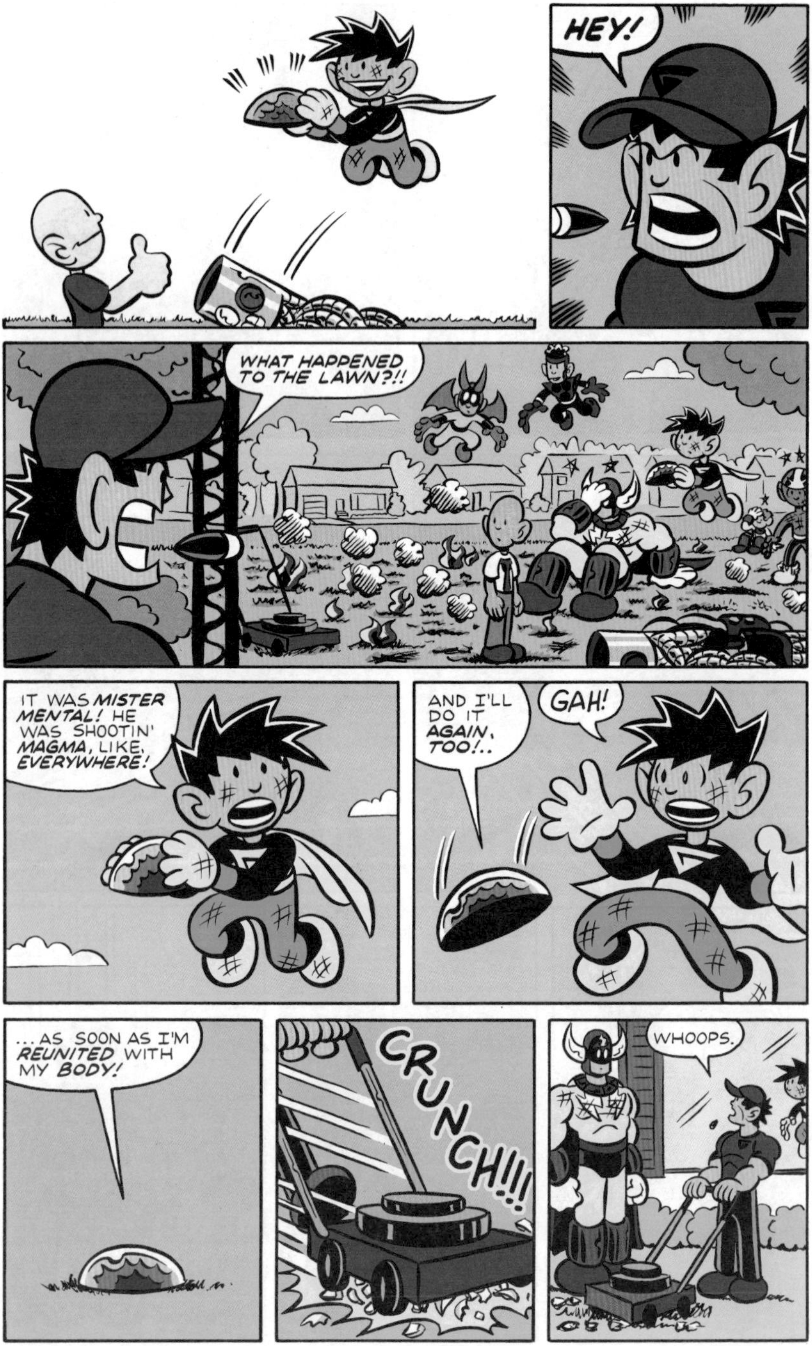
HEY!
WHAT HAPPENED TO THE LAWN?!!
IT WAS MISTER MENTAL! HE WAS SHOOTIN' MAGMA, LIKE, EVERYWHERE!
AND I'LL DO IT AGAIN, TOO!..
GAH!
...AS SOON AS I'M REUNITED WITH MY BODY!
CRUNCH!!!
WHOOPS.

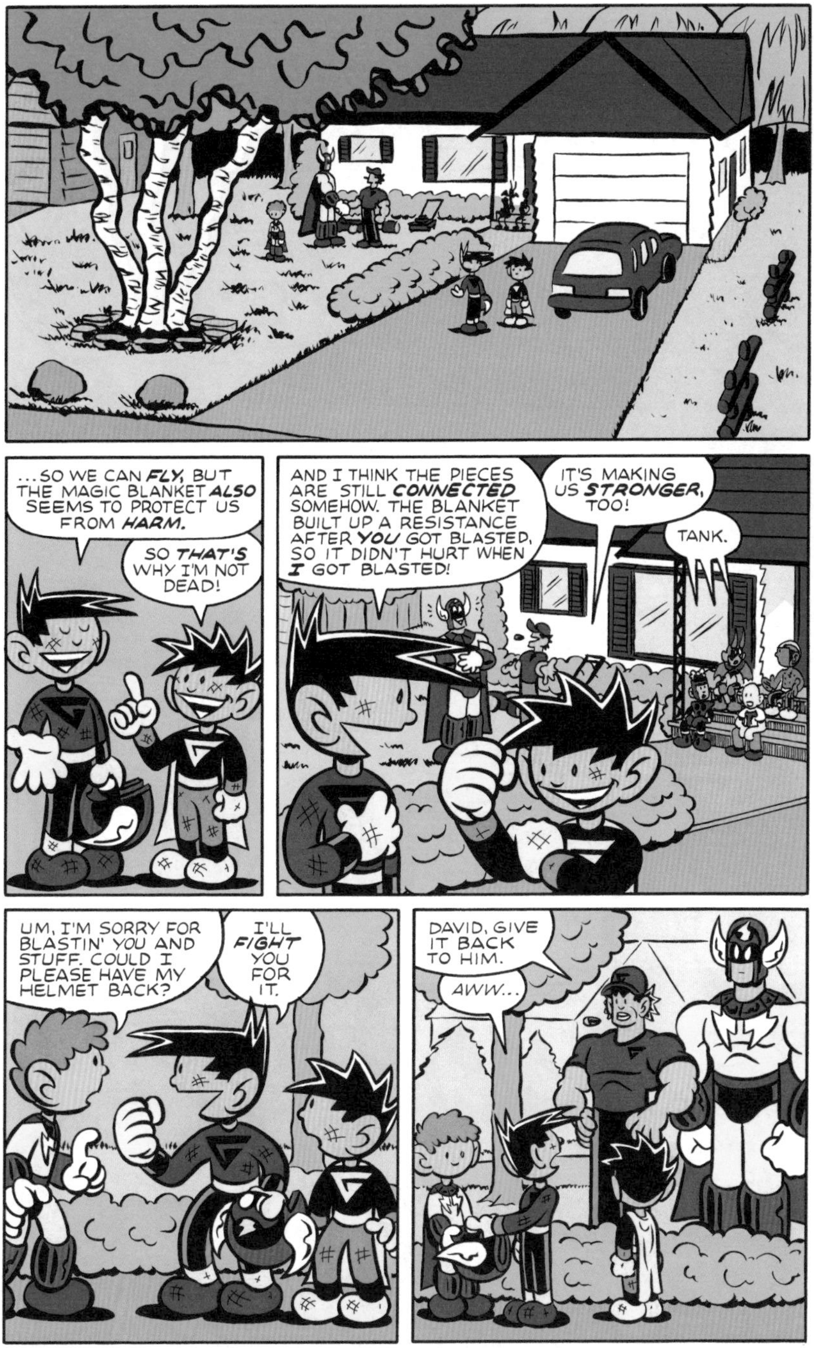
...SO WE CAN FLY, BUT THE MAGIC BLANKET ALSO SEEMS TO PROTECT US FROM HARM.
SO THAT'S WHY I'M NOT DEAD!
AND I THINK THE PIECES ARE STILL CONNECTED SOMEHOW. THE BLANKET BUILT UP A RESISTANCE AFTER YOU GOT BLASTED, SO IT DIDN'T HURT WHEN I GOT BLASTED!
IT'S MAKING US STRONGER, TOO!
TANK.
UM, I'M SORRY FOR BLASTIN' YOU AND STUFF. COULD I PLEASE HAVE MY HELMET BACK?
I'LL FIGHT YOU FOR IT.
DAVID, GIVE IT BACK TO HIM.
AWW...

IT'S COMING ON! HERE IT IS!

CAPTAIN THUNDERMAN SAVED THE CITY YET AGAIN THIS AFTERNOON WHEN HE RE-DEFEATED MISTER MENTAL, WHO HAD JUST RETURNED FROM THE DEAD.

HE DIDN'T DO IT ALONE THOUGH. HIS SON, KID THUNDER, WAS THERE TO LEND A HELPING HAND! IN OTHER NEWS...

WHAT ABOUT US? WE SAVED THE DAY! WE STOPPED MISTER MENTAL WHEN CAPTAIN THUNDERMAN WAS DOWN!

OF COURSE YOU DID, HONEY.

DAD, WHY--

BECAUSE I ASKED CAPTAIN THUNDERMAN TO REPORT IT THAT WAY. I DON'T NEED MISTER MENTAL'S SUPER PSYCHO FRIENDS COMING BY TO EXACT REVENGE OR GO TEARING UP THE LAWN!

DAVE, CAN YOU BELIEVE THIS?

...

WHERE'S DAVE?

HE'S PLAYING VIDEO GAMES OVER AT HIS FRIEND'S HOUSE.

WHO?

THE END

MEAN BROTHER COMICS by G-man

Idiot Brother Comics by GREAT MAN

BULLET DODGING DRILLS?

Y'KNOW, GUYS, I DIDN'T NEED TO COME TO THIS *CAMP* TO GET SHOT UP.

I COULD HAVE HAD THE *MARKSMAN* SHOOT ME FOR *FREE* AND I WOULDN'T HAVE HAD TO WAIT IN *LINE, EITHER!*

WHY COULDN'T WE HAVE LEARNED THE *INVULNERABILITY* DRILL FIRST?

G, YOU'LL FEEL BETTER AFTER THE ACCELERATED HEALING DRILL. WE'LL WAIT OUT HERE.

TRAINER

SHOT UP IN THE BULLET CAGE, EH? BETTER PUT SOME *ICE* ON THAT.

THAT'S IT?

TRAINER

HERE, DRINK SOME OF THIS *MAGIC POTION HEALTH SUPPLEMENT*, TOO. I GET IT FROM A KID WHO RUNS A LEMONADE STAND.

RAIN

IT'S GOOD STUFF. IT PROMOTES *ACCELERATED HEALING* AND *RECOVERY,* WHILE BOOSTING YOUR *STRENGTH* AND *ENERGY.*

WOULDN'T IT HAVE TO STAY IN MY BODY IN ORDER TO WORK?

TRAINER

HEY, LET'S GO CHECK OUT THE GIRLS WORKING ON THEIR EYE BEAM DRILLS OVER THERE.

LOOKING GOOD, *LITHICORE!*

COACH

YOUR *COSMIC STARE* IS IMPROVING, *STARGAZE!*

COACH

C'MON, *MAGMA!* YOU'VE ALMOST *GOT* IT! WHAT'S *WRONG?*

UHN...

COAC

MY *CONTACT LENSES* ARE MELTING!

COACH

C'MON, LET'S GO SEE HOW G-MAN'S DOING.

COACH

HOW ARE YOU FEELING, G?

GREAT! THAT MAGIC POTION REALLY HEALED MY BODY...

...BUT I THINK MAYBE I DRANK TOO MUCH.

CG '02

COMIC BITS BY CHRIS GIARRUSSO

COACH

SSSC

COACH

NOW THAT THE BANQUET IS DRAWING TO A CLOSE, I JUST WANT TO SAY ON BEHALF OF ALL OF THE COACHES HERE, THAT YOU HAVE BEEN A GREAT GROUP OF KIDS TO WORK WITH THIS SUMMER.

ONCE AGAIN, I'D LIKE TO THANK *G.I. SMILEY*, THE ORIGINAL *HAPPY HERO*, FOR JOINING US AS OUR GUEST SPEAKER THIS EVENING. LET'S HEAR IT FOR HIM!

COACH

CLAP CLAP CLAP CLAP CLAP C

BEFORE YOU GO, THOSE OF YOU WHO ORDERED *T-SHIRTS* DURING CAMP REGISTRATION CAN PICK UP YOUR SHIRTS AT THE BACK TABLE.

T-SHIRTS, BABY, *T-SHIRTS!*

THEY'VE GOT OUR SNAZZY *SUNNYSIDE SUPER HERO SUMMER CAMP* LOGO ON THE BACK, AND YOUR NAME WILL BE ON THE FRONT.

SSSC

I CAN'T BELIEVE IT'S THE *LAST DAY OF CAMP!*

I KNOW! I NEVER EVEN GOT A CHANCE TO MEET THAT CUTE *G-MAN!*

?

LET'S SEE... AH, HERE WE ARE --- *G-MAN!*

G-MAN

ENJOY YOUR NEW T-SHIRT, *G-MAN!*

THANK YOU!

T-SHIRTS

WHAT THE -- ?

J-MAN

G-MAN! YOU GOT YOUR *SHIRT?*

YEAH... BUT THEY SPELLED MY *NAME* WRONG.

BILLY DEMON

G

WHAT? HOW DID THEY MISSPELL *"G-MAN"?*

THEY SPELLED THE *"G"* WRONG.

THAT'S AN UNDERSTANDABLE MISTAKE -- IT'S *HARD* TO SPELL THE LETTER *"G".*

YO, "G" IS LIKE, ONE OF THE MOST DIFFICULT LETTERS TO *SPELL*.

SOMETIMES I FORRET THERE'S EVEN A LETTER "G" IN THE *ALPHABET!*

TAN MAN

SPARK

TREE MAN

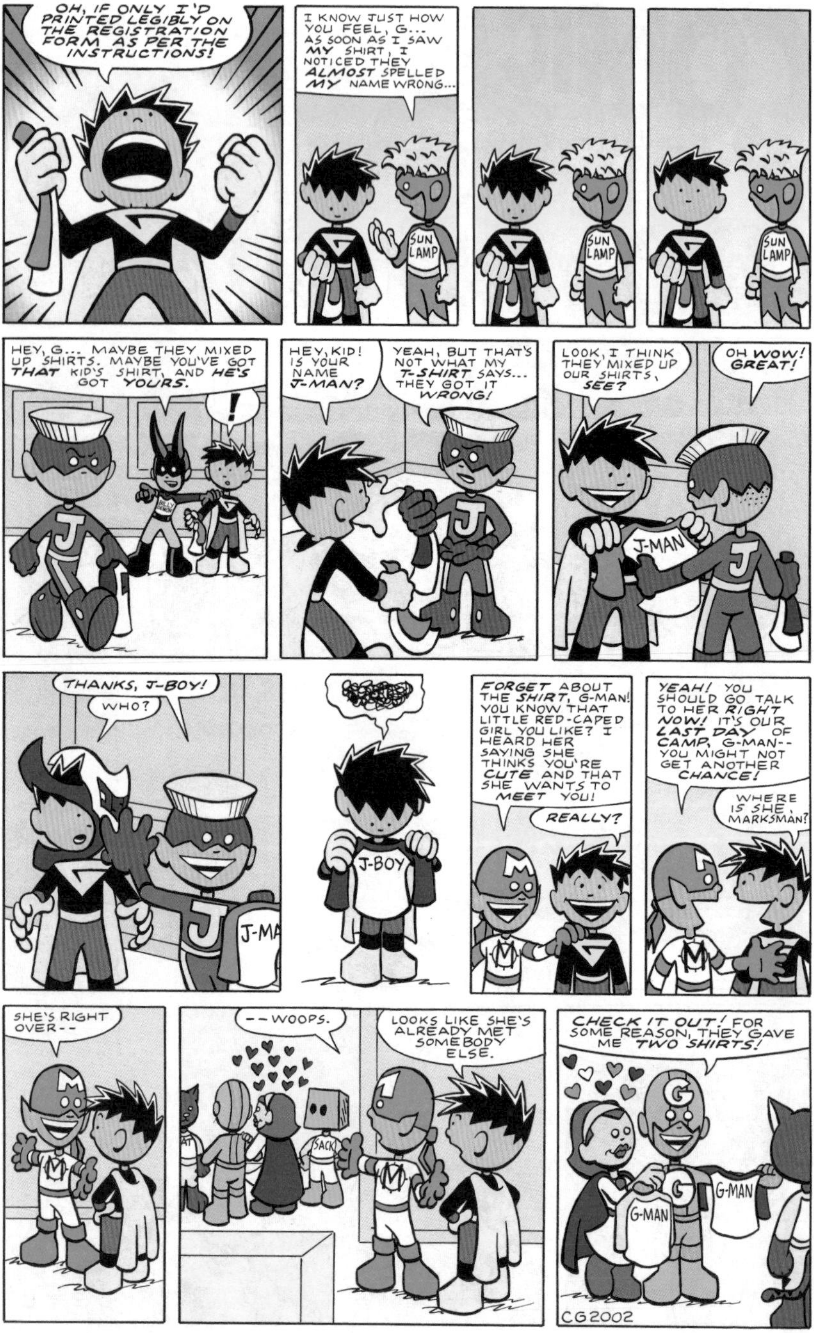
OH, IF ONLY I'D PRINTED LEGIBLY ON THE REGISTRATION FORM AS PER THE INSTRUCTIONS!
I KNOW JUST HOW YOU FEEL, G... AS SOON AS I SAW MY SHIRT, I NOTICED THEY ALMOST SPELLED MY NAME WRONG...
SUN LAMP
HEY, G... MAYBE THEY MIXED UP SHIRTS. MAYBE YOU'VE GOT THAT KID'S SHIRT, AND HE'S GOT YOURS.
!
HEY, KID! IS YOUR NAME J-MAN?
YEAH, BUT THAT'S NOT WHAT MY T-SHIRT SAYS... THEY GOT IT WRONG!
LOOK, I THINK THEY MIXED UP OUR SHIRTS, SEE?
OH WOW! GREAT!
J-MAN
THANKS, J-BOY!
WHO?
J-MA
J-BOY
FORGET ABOUT THE SHIRT, G-MAN! YOU KNOW THAT LITTLE RED-CAPED GIRL YOU LIKE? I HEARD HER SAYING SHE THINKS YOU'RE CUTE AND THAT SHE WANTS TO MEET YOU!
REALLY?
YEAH! YOU SHOULD GO TALK TO HER RIGHT NOW! IT'S OUR LAST DAY OF CAMP, G-MAN-- YOU MIGHT NOT GET ANOTHER CHANCE!
WHERE IS SHE, MARKSMAN?
SHE'S RIGHT OVER--
--WOOPS.
SACK
LOOKS LIKE SHE'S ALREADY MET SOMEBODY ELSE.
CHECK IT OUT! FOR SOME REASON, THEY GAVE ME TWO SHIRTS!
G-MAN
G-MAN
CG2002

BY CHRIS GIARRUSSO

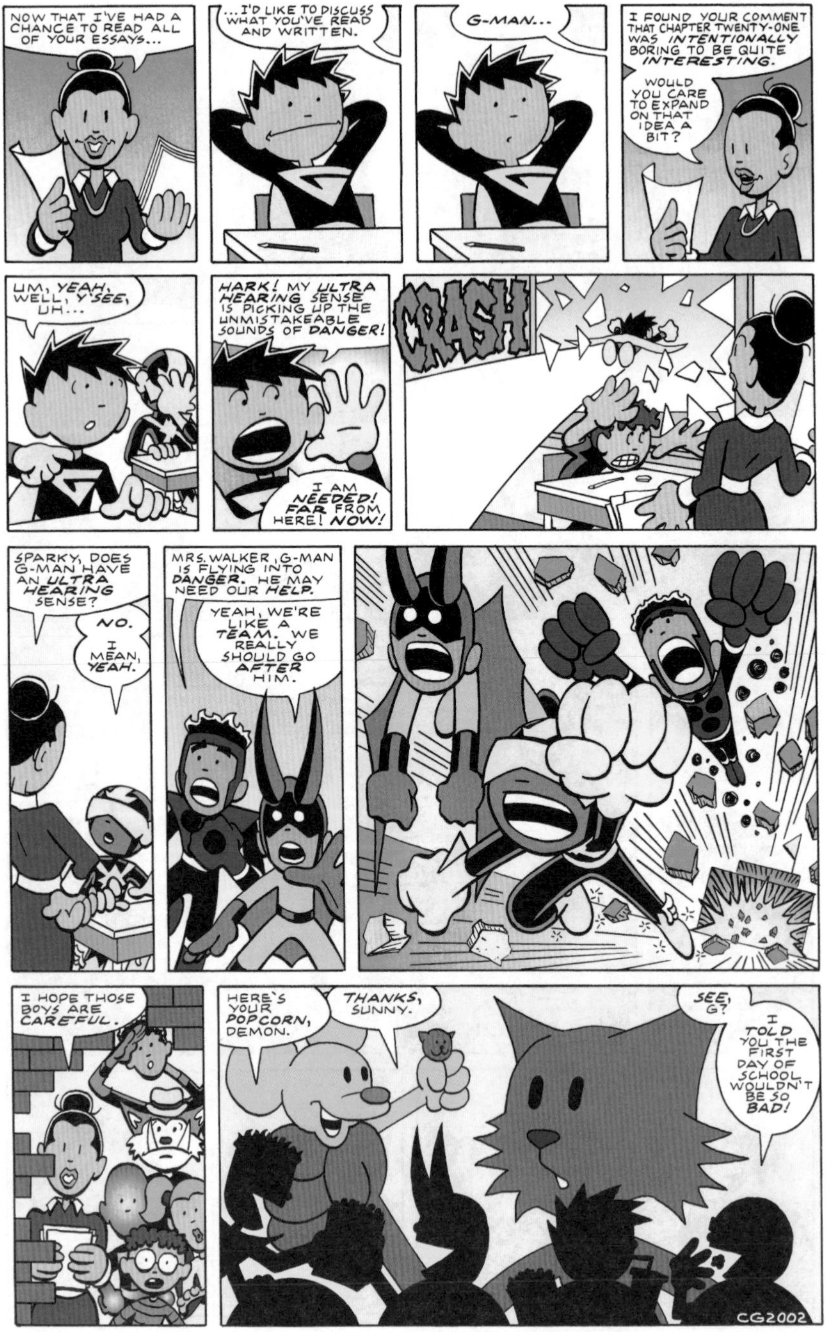
NOW THAT I'VE HAD A CHANCE TO READ ALL OF YOUR ESSAYS...
...I'D LIKE TO DISCUSS WHAT YOU'VE READ AND WRITTEN.
G-MAN...
I FOUND YOUR COMMENT THAT CHAPTER TWENTY-ONE WAS INTENTIONALLY BORING TO BE QUITE INTERESTING.
WOULD YOU CARE TO EXPAND ON THAT IDEA A BIT?
UM, YEAH, WELL, Y'SEE, UH...
HARK! MY ULTRA HEARING SENSE IS PICKING UP THE UNMISTAKEABLE SOUNDS OF DANGER!
I AM NEEDED! FAR FROM HERE! NOW!
CRASH
SPARKY, DOES G-MAN HAVE AN ULTRA HEARING SENSE?
NO.
I MEAN, YEAH.
MRS. WALKER, G-MAN IS FLYING INTO DANGER. HE MAY NEED OUR HELP.
YEAH, WE'RE LIKE A TEAM. WE REALLY SHOULD GO AFTER HIM.
I HOPE THOSE BOYS ARE CAREFUL.
HERE'S YOUR POPCORN, DEMON.
THANKS, SUNNY.
SEE, G?
I TOLD YOU THE FIRST DAY OF SCHOOL WOULDN'T BE SO BAD!
CG2002

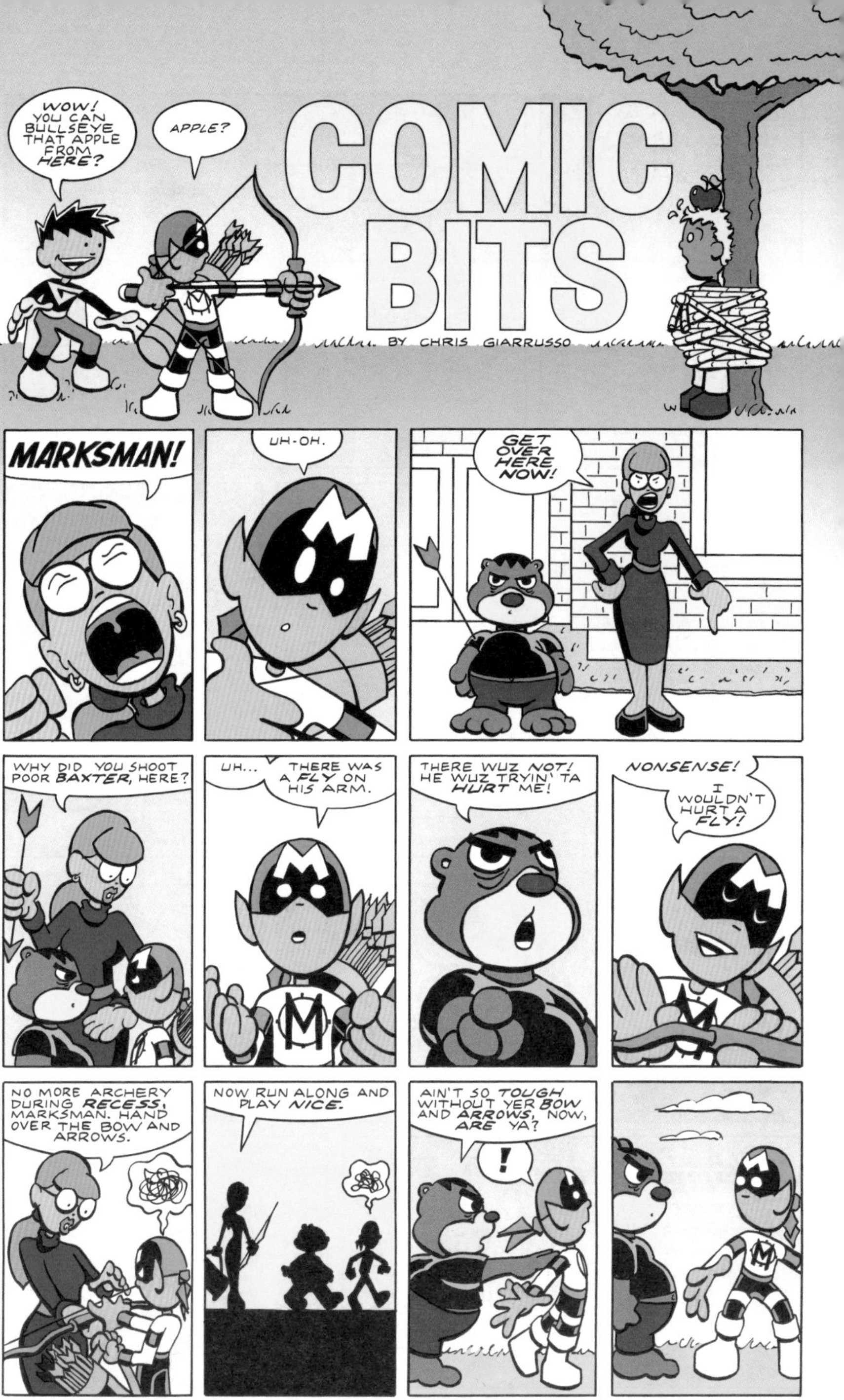
WOW! YOU CAN BULLSEYE THAT APPLE FROM HERE?
APPLE?
COMIC BITS
BY CHRIS GIARRUSSO
MARKSMAN!
UH-OH.
GET OVER HERE NOW!
WHY DID YOU SHOOT POOR BAXTER, HERE?
UH...
THERE WAS A FLY ON HIS ARM.
THERE WUZ NOT! HE WUZ TRYIN' TA HURT ME!
NONSENSE!
I WOULDN'T HURT A FLY!
NO MORE ARCHERY DURING RECESS, MARKSMAN. HAND OVER THE BOW AND ARROWS.
NOW RUN ALONG AND PLAY NICE.
AIN'T SO TOUGH WITHOUT YER BOW AND ARROWS, NOW, ARE YA?
!

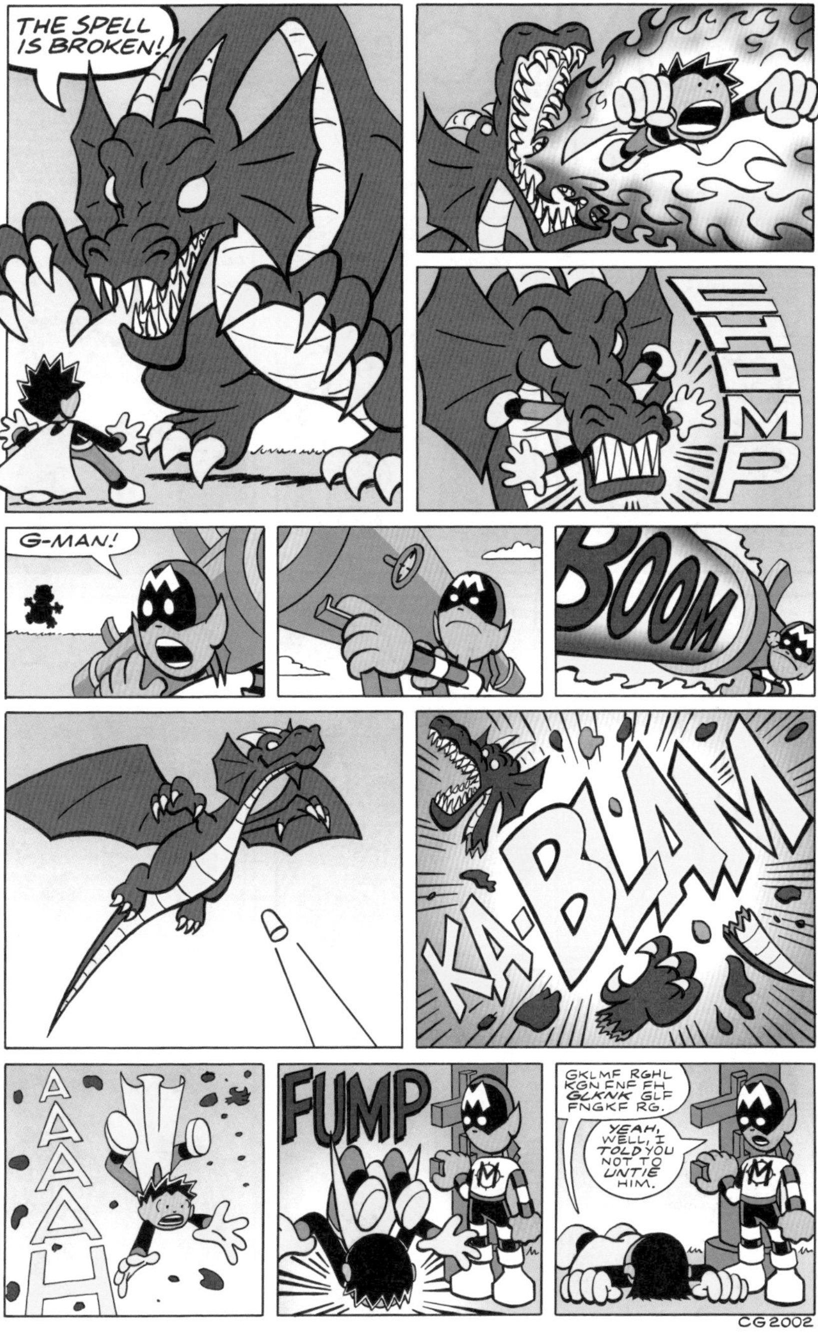
THE SPELL IS BROKEN!
CHOMP
G-MAN!
BOOM
KA-BLAM
AAAAAH
FUMP
GKLMF RGHL KGN FNF FH GLKNK GLF FNGKF RG.
YEAH, WELL, I TOLD YOU NOT TO UNTIE HIM.
CG2002

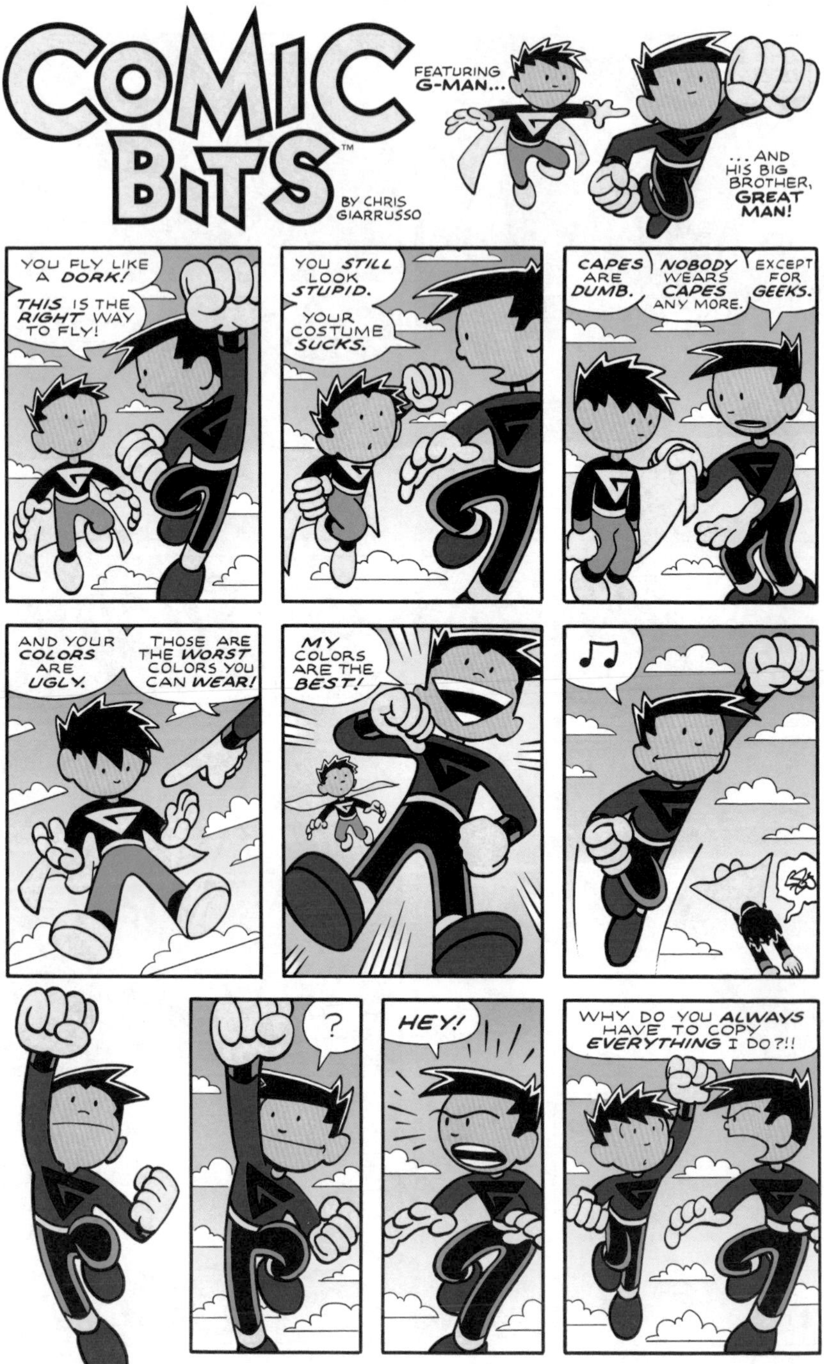
COMIC BITS™
FEATURING G-MAN...
...AND HIS BIG BROTHER, GREAT MAN!
BY CHRIS GIARRUSSO
YOU FLY LIKE A DORK!
THIS IS THE RIGHT WAY TO FLY!
YOU STILL LOOK STUPID.
YOUR COSTUME SUCKS.
CAPES ARE DUMB.
NOBODY WEARS CAPES ANY MORE.
EXCEPT FOR GEEKS.
AND YOUR COLORS ARE UGLY.
THOSE ARE THE WORST COLORS YOU CAN WEAR!
MY COLORS ARE THE BEST!
♫
?
HEY!
WHY DO YOU ALWAYS HAVE TO COPY EVERYTHING I DO?!!

MEAN BROTHER COMICS

by G-man

Idiot Brother Comics

by GREAT MAN

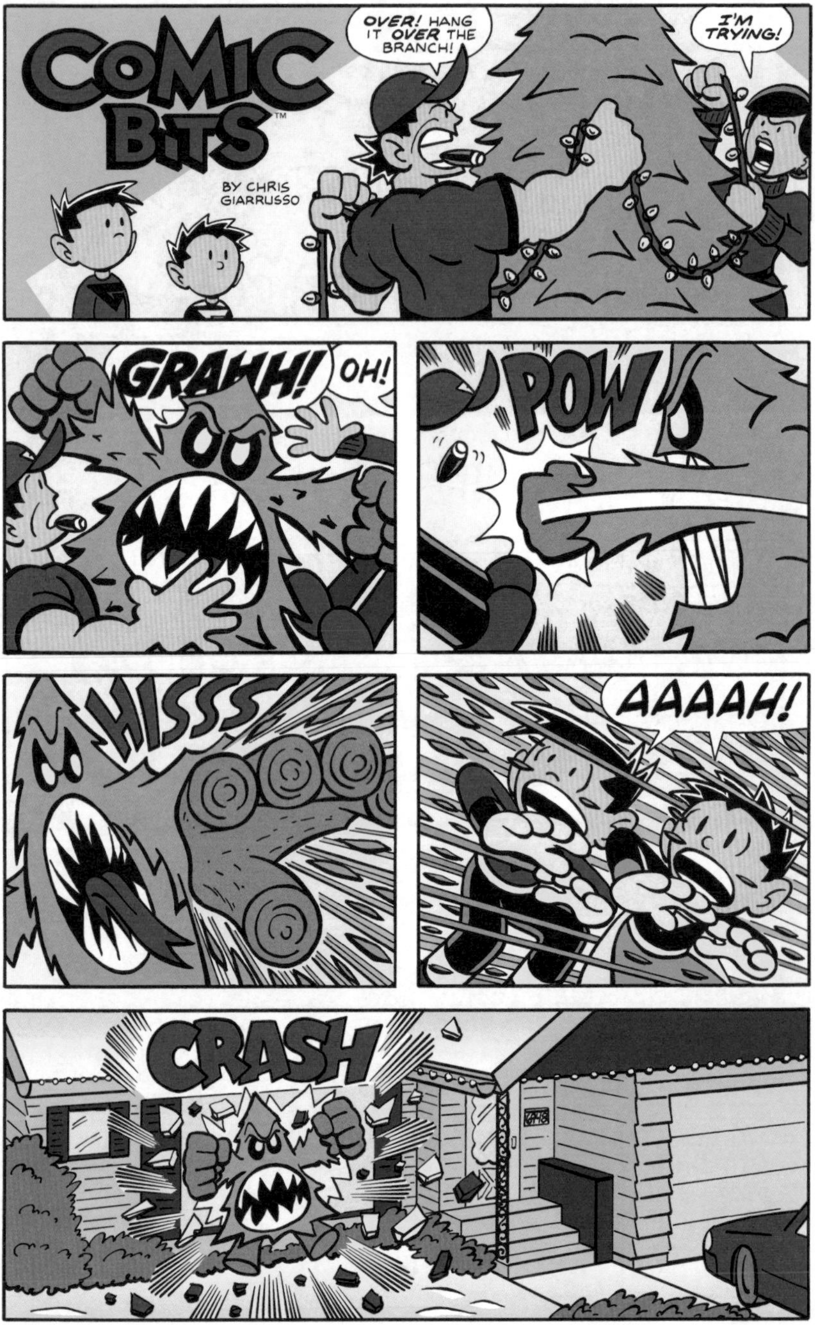
COMIC BITS™
BY CHRIS GIARRUSSO
OVER! HANG IT OVER THE BRANCH!
I'M TRYING!
GRAHH!
OH!
POW
HISSS
AAAAH!
CRASH

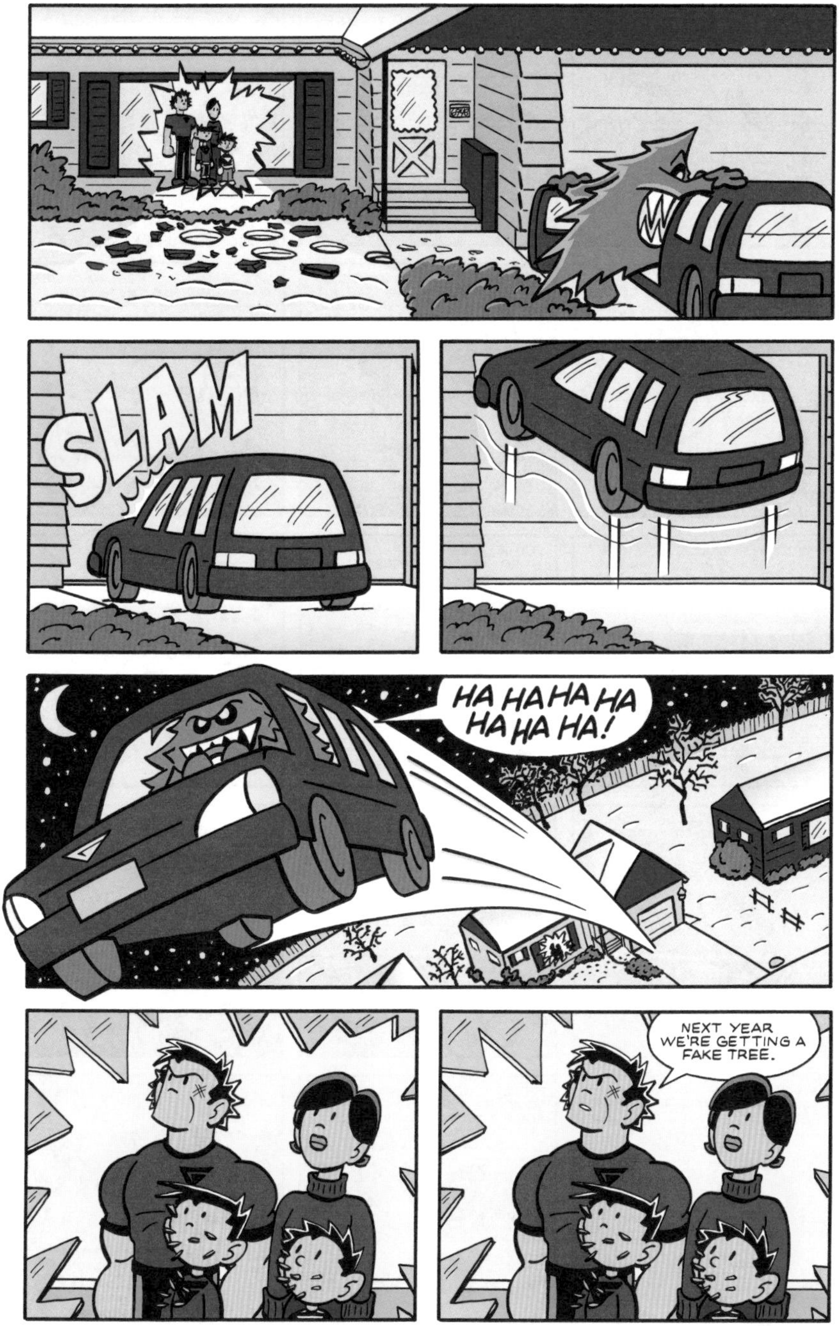
SLAM
HA HA HA HA HA HA HA HA!
NEXT YEAR WE'RE GETTING A FAKE TREE.

G-MAN™ and the Christmas Tree of Doom

by Chris Giarrusso

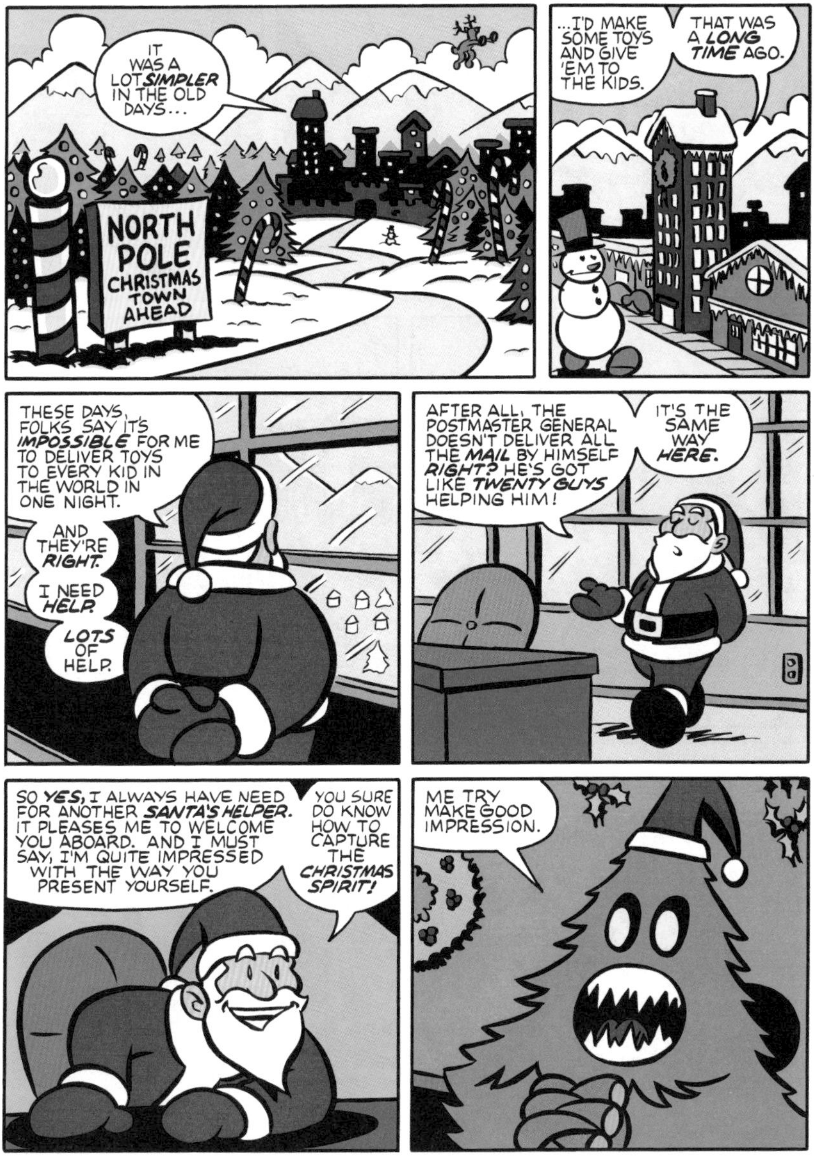
IT WAS A LOT SIMPLER IN THE OLD DAYS...
NORTH POLE CHRISTMAS TOWN AHEAD
...I'D MAKE SOME TOYS AND GIVE 'EM TO THE KIDS.
THAT WAS A LONG TIME AGO.
THESE DAYS, FOLKS SAY IT'S IMPOSSIBLE FOR ME TO DELIVER TOYS TO EVERY KID IN THE WORLD IN ONE NIGHT.
AND THEY'RE RIGHT.
I NEED HELP.
LOTS OF HELP.
AFTER ALL, THE POSTMASTER GENERAL DOESN'T DELIVER ALL THE MAIL BY HIMSELF RIGHT? HE'S GOT LIKE TWENTY GUYS HELPING HIM!
IT'S THE SAME WAY HERE.
SO YES, I ALWAYS HAVE NEED FOR ANOTHER SANTA'S HELPER. IT PLEASES ME TO WELCOME YOU ABOARD. AND I MUST SAY, I'M QUITE IMPRESSED WITH THE WAY YOU PRESENT YOURSELF.
YOU SURE DO KNOW HOW TO CAPTURE THE CHRISTMAS SPIRIT!
ME TRY MAKE GOOD IMPRESSION.

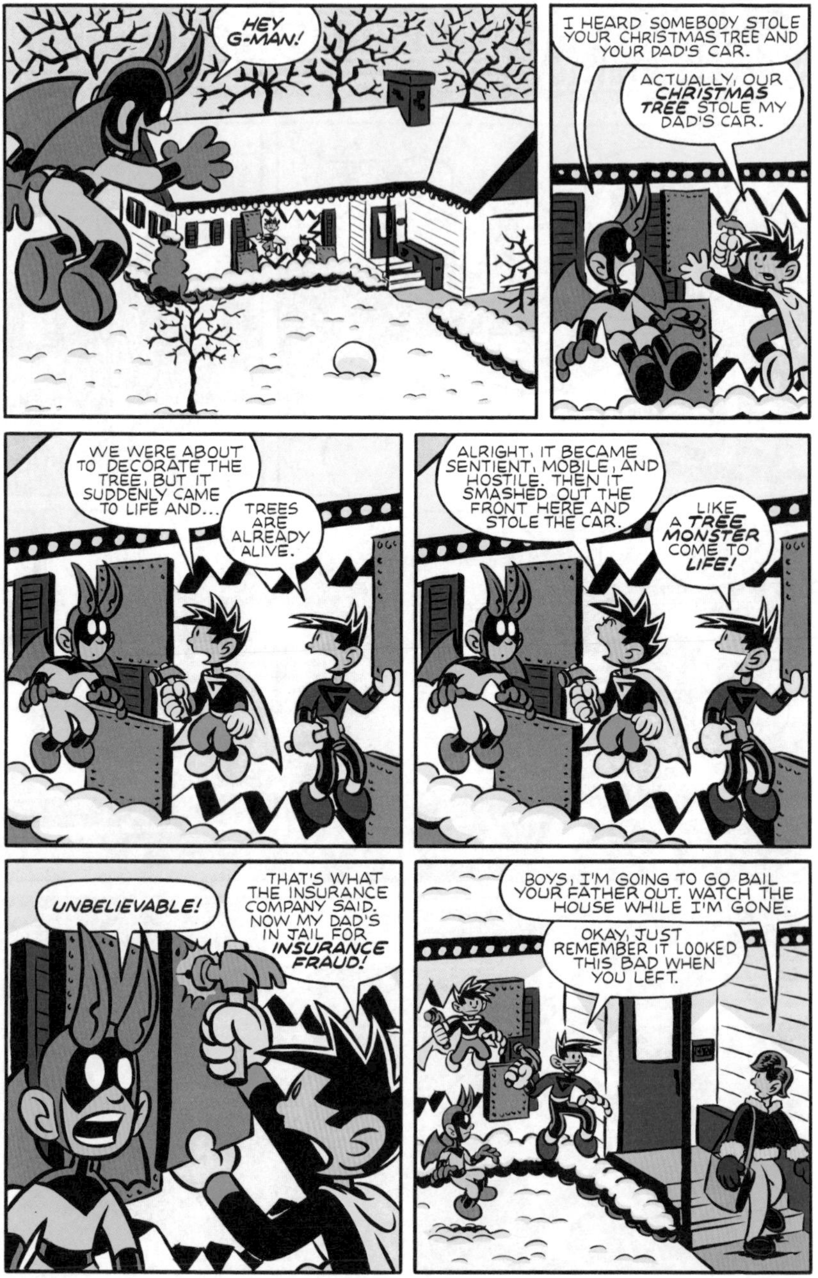
HEY G-MAN!
I HEARD SOMEBODY STOLE YOUR CHRISTMAS TREE AND YOUR DAD'S CAR.
ACTUALLY, OUR CHRISTMAS TREE STOLE MY DAD'S CAR.
WE WERE ABOUT TO DECORATE THE TREE, BUT IT SUDDENLY CAME TO LIFE AND...
TREES ARE ALREADY ALIVE.
ALRIGHT, IT BECAME SENTIENT, MOBILE, AND HOSTILE. THEN IT SMASHED OUT THE FRONT HERE AND STOLE THE CAR.
LIKE A TREE MONSTER COME TO LIFE!
UNBELIEVABLE!
THAT'S WHAT THE INSURANCE COMPANY SAID. NOW MY DAD'S IN JAIL FOR INSURANCE FRAUD!
BOYS, I'M GOING TO GO BAIL YOUR FATHER OUT. WATCH THE HOUSE WHILE I'M GONE.
OKAY, JUST REMEMBER IT LOOKED THIS BAD WHEN YOU LEFT.

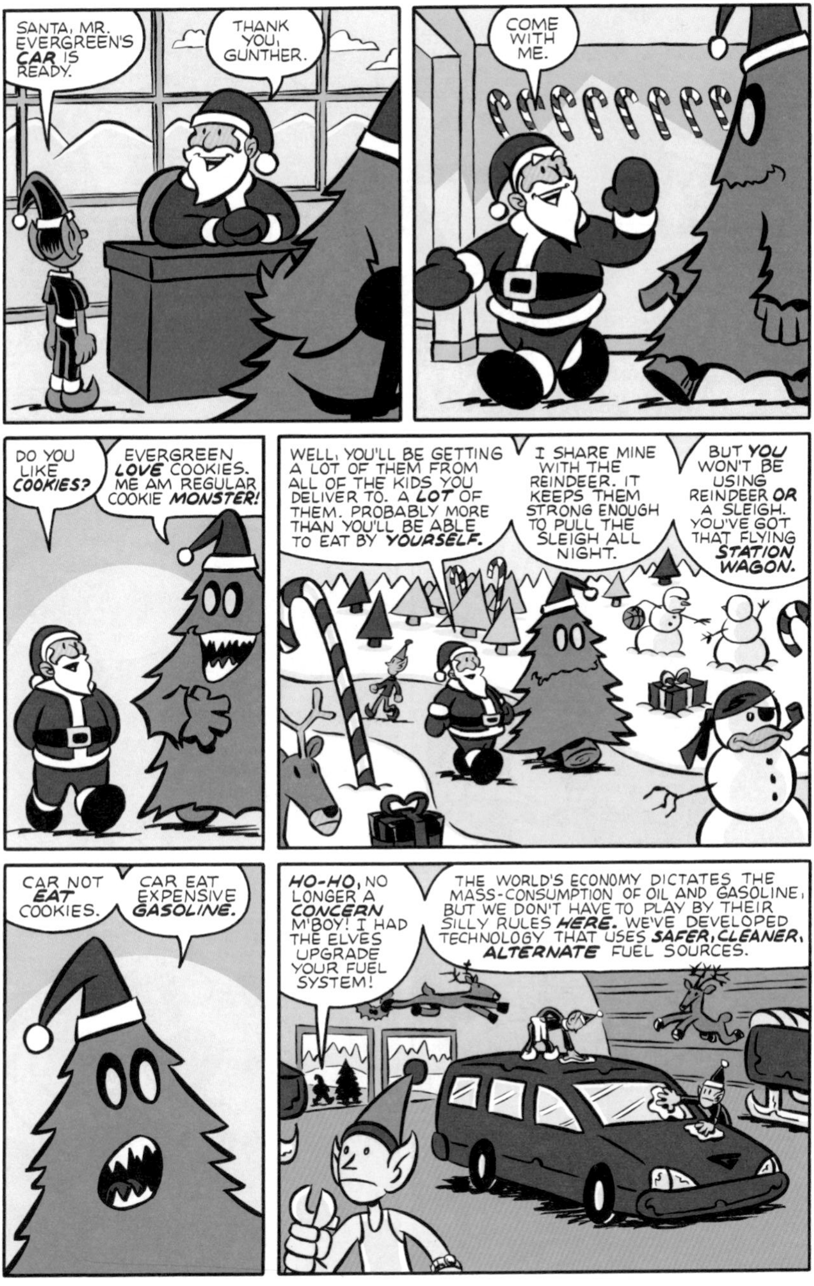

SANTA, MR. EVERGREEN'S **CAR** IS READY.
THANK YOU, GUNTHER.
COME WITH ME.
DO YOU LIKE **COOKIES?**
EVERGREEN **LOVE** COOKIES. ME AM REGULAR COOKIE **MONSTER!**
WELL, YOU'LL BE GETTING A LOT OF THEM FROM ALL OF THE KIDS YOU DELIVER TO. A **LOT** OF THEM. PROBABLY MORE THAN YOU'LL BE ABLE TO EAT BY **YOURSELF.**
I SHARE MINE WITH THE REINDEER. IT KEEPS THEM STRONG ENOUGH TO PULL THE SLEIGH ALL NIGHT.
BUT **YOU** WON'T BE USING REINDEER **OR** A SLEIGH. YOU'VE GOT THAT FLYING **STATION WAGON.**
CAR NOT **EAT** COOKIES.
CAR EAT EXPENSIVE **GASOLINE.**
HO-HO, NO LONGER A **CONCERN** M'BOY! I HAD THE ELVES UPGRADE YOUR FUEL SYSTEM!
THE WORLD'S ECONOMY DICTATES THE MASS-CONSUMPTION OF OIL AND GASOLINE, BUT WE DON'T HAVE TO PLAY BY THEIR SILLY RULES **HERE.** WE'VE DEVELOPED TECHNOLOGY THAT USES **SAFER, CLEANER, ALTERNATE** FUEL SOURCES.

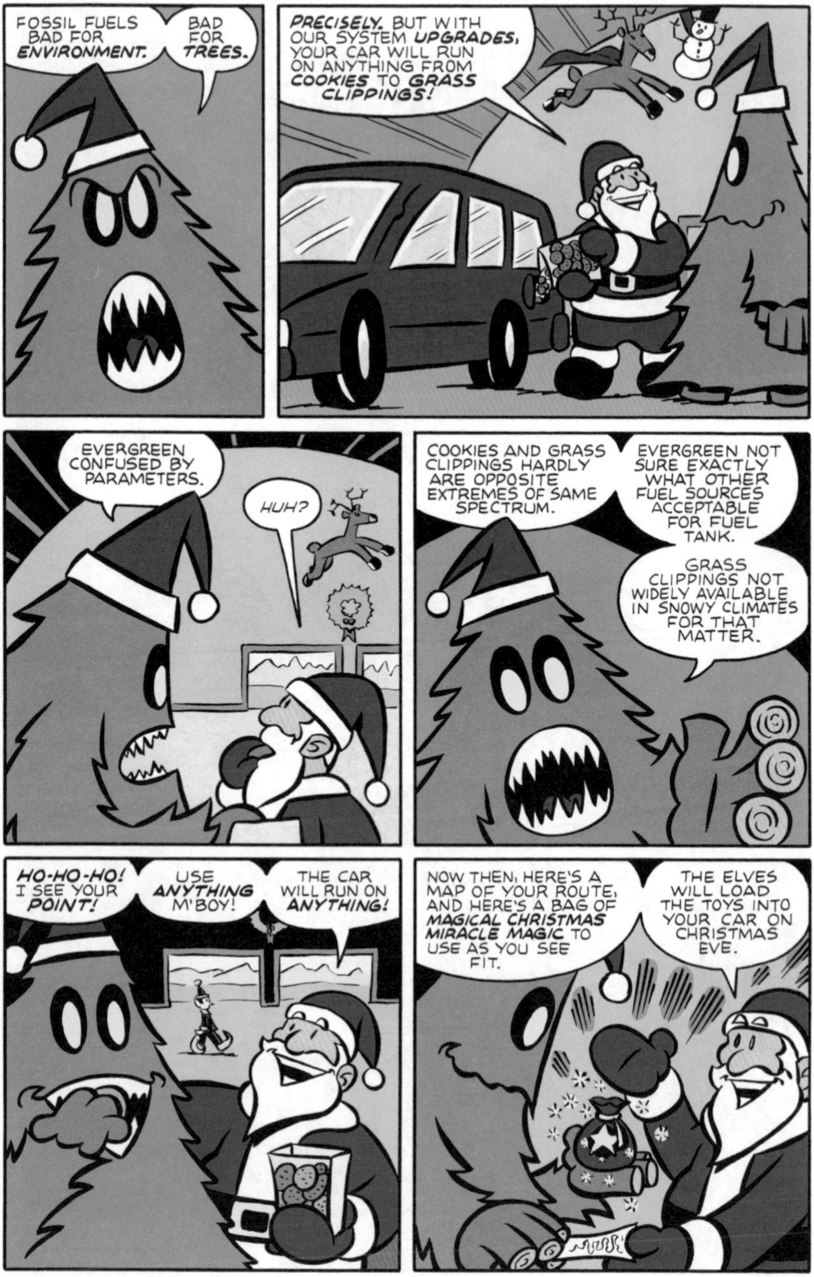
FOSSIL FUELS BAD FOR ENVIRONMENT.
BAD FOR TREES.
PRECISELY. BUT WITH OUR SYSTEM UPGRADES, YOUR CAR WILL RUN ON ANYTHING FROM COOKIES TO GRASS CLIPPINGS!
EVERGREEN CONFUSED BY PARAMETERS.
HUH?
COOKIES AND GRASS CLIPPINGS HARDLY ARE OPPOSITE EXTREMES OF SAME SPECTRUM.
EVERGREEN NOT SURE EXACTLY WHAT OTHER FUEL SOURCES ACCEPTABLE FOR FUEL TANK.
GRASS CLIPPINGS NOT WIDELY AVAILABLE IN SNOWY CLIMATES FOR THAT MATTER.
HO-HO-HO! I SEE YOUR POINT!
USE ANYTHING M'BOY!
THE CAR WILL RUN ON ANYTHING!
NOW THEN, HERE'S A MAP OF YOUR ROUTE, AND HERE'S A BAG OF MAGICAL CHRISTMAS MIRACLE MAGIC TO USE AS YOU SEE FIT.
THE ELVES WILL LOAD THE TOYS INTO YOUR CAR ON CHRISTMAS EVE.

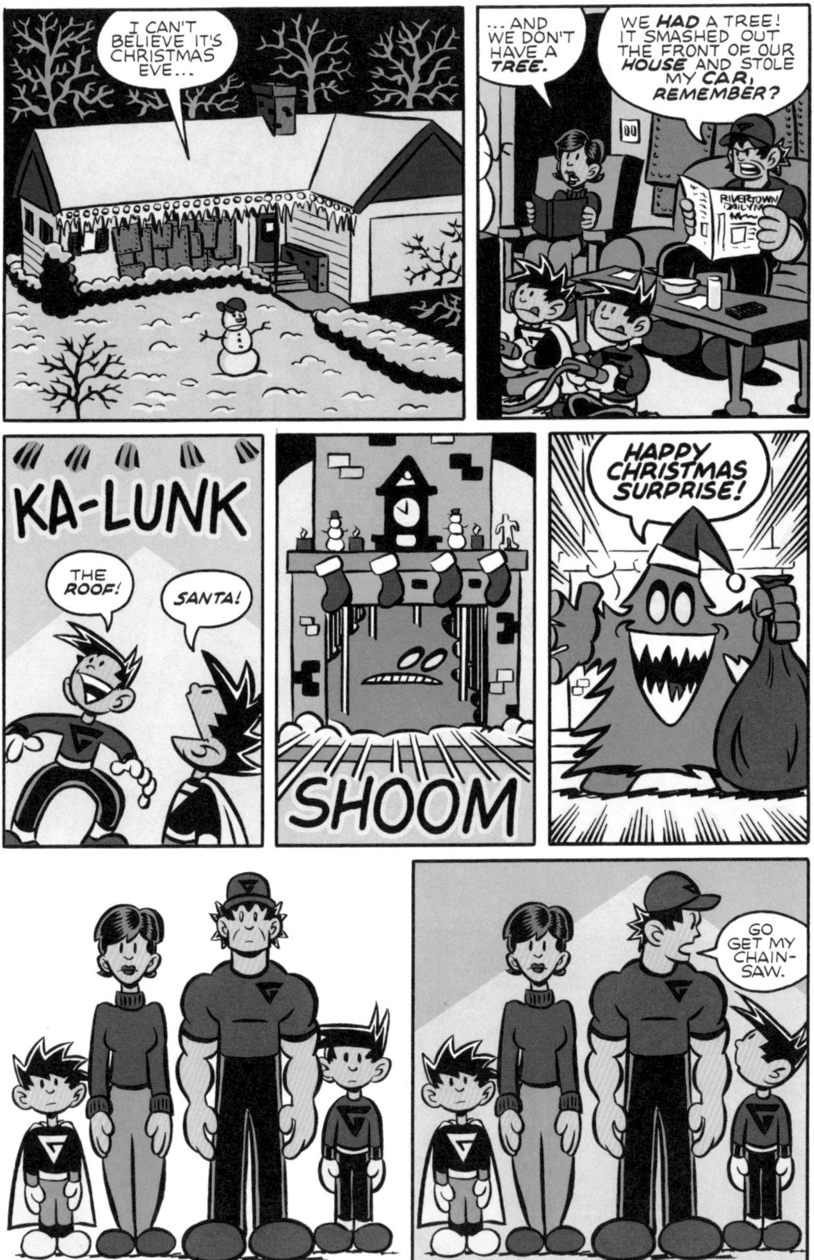
I CAN'T BELIEVE IT'S CHRISTMAS EVE...
...AND WE DON'T HAVE A TREE.
WE HAD A TREE! IT SMASHED OUT THE FRONT OF OUR HOUSE AND STOLE MY CAR, REMEMBER?
RIVERTOWN DAILY
KA-LUNK
THE ROOF!
SANTA!
SHOOM
HAPPY CHRISTMAS SURPRISE!
GO GET MY CHAIN-SAW.

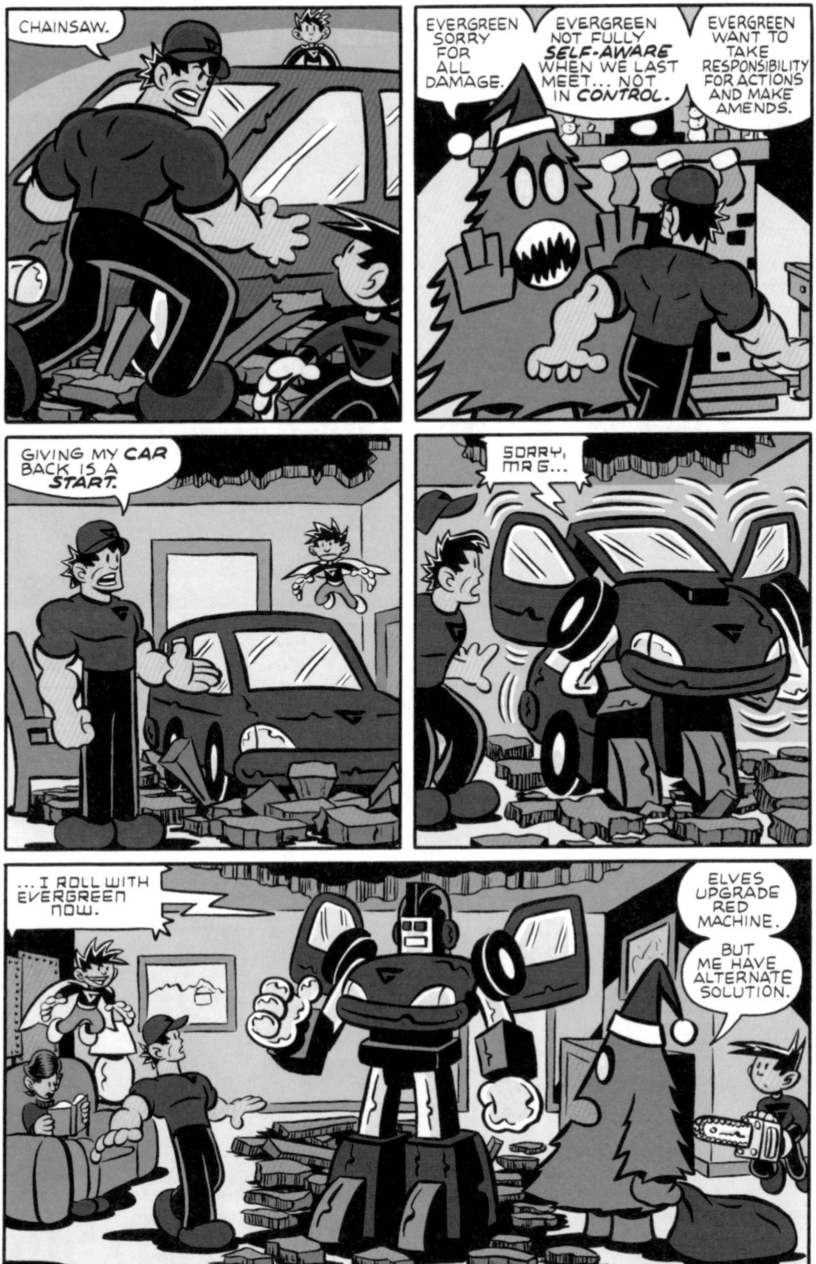
CHAINSAW.
EVERGREEN SORRY FOR ALL DAMAGE.
EVERGREEN NOT FULLY SELF-AWARE WHEN WE LAST MEET... NOT IN CONTROL.
EVERGREEN WANT TO TAKE RESPONSIBILITY FOR ACTIONS AND MAKE AMENDS.
GIVING MY CAR BACK IS A START.
SORRY, MR G...
...I ROLL WITH EVERGREEN NOW.
ELVES UPGRADE RED MACHINE.
BUT ME HAVE ALTERNATE SOLUTION.

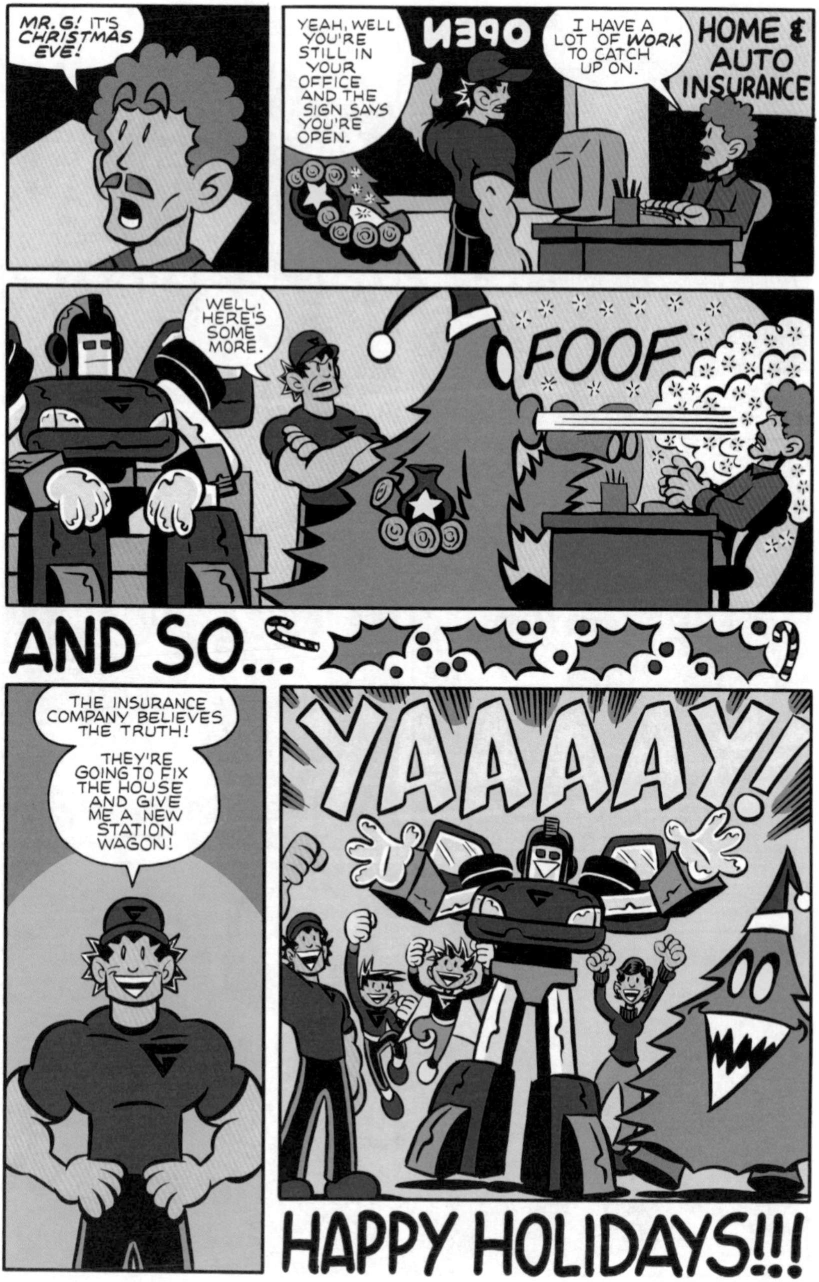

MR. G! IT'S CHRISTMAS EVE!
YEAH, WELL YOU'RE STILL IN YOUR OFFICE AND THE SIGN SAYS YOU'RE OPEN.
OPEN
I HAVE A LOT OF WORK TO CATCH UP ON.
HOME & AUTO INSURANCE
WELL, HERE'S SOME MORE.
FOOF
AND SO...
THE INSURANCE COMPANY BELIEVES THE TRUTH!
THEY'RE GOING TO FIX THE HOUSE AND GIVE ME A NEW STATION WAGON!
YAAAAY!
HAPPY HOLIDAYS!!!

MEAN BROTHER COMICS by G-man

Idiot Brother Comics by GREAT MAN

BY CHRIS GIARRUSSO

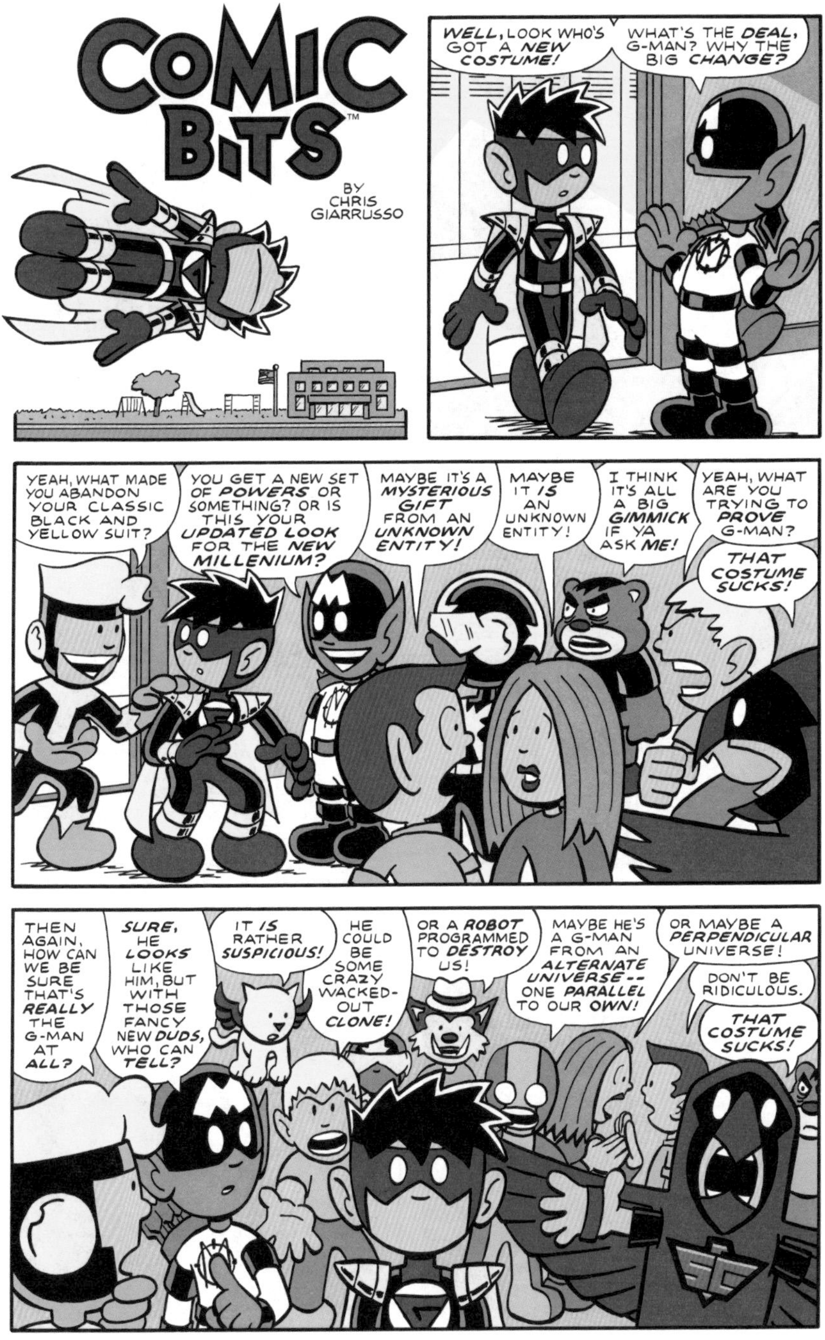
COMIC BITS™
BY CHRIS GIARRUSSO
WELL, LOOK WHO'S GOT A NEW COSTUME!
WHAT'S THE DEAL, G-MAN? WHY THE BIG CHANGE?
YEAH, WHAT MADE YOU ABANDON YOUR CLASSIC BLACK AND YELLOW SUIT?
YOU GET A NEW SET OF POWERS OR SOMETHING? OR IS THIS YOUR UPDATED LOOK FOR THE NEW MILLENIUM?
MAYBE IT'S A MYSTERIOUS GIFT FROM AN UNKNOWN ENTITY!
MAYBE IT IS AN UNKNOWN ENTITY!
I THINK IT'S ALL A BIG GIMMICK IF YA ASK ME!
YEAH, WHAT ARE YOU TRYING TO PROVE G-MAN?
THAT COSTUME SUCKS!
THEN AGAIN, HOW CAN WE BE SURE THAT'S REALLY THE G-MAN AT ALL?
SURE, HE LOOKS LIKE HIM, BUT WITH THOSE FANCY NEW DUDS, WHO CAN TELL?
IT IS RATHER SUSPICIOUS!
HE COULD BE SOME CRAZY WACKED-OUT CLONE!
OR A ROBOT PROGRAMMED TO DESTROY US!
MAYBE HE'S A G-MAN FROM AN ALTERNATE UNIVERSE-- ONE PARALLEL TO OUR OWN!
OR MAYBE A PERPENDICULAR UNIVERSE!
DON'T BE RIDICULOUS.
THAT COSTUME SUCKS!

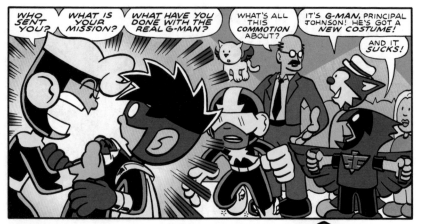

WHO SENT YOU?

WHAT IS YOUR MISSION?

WHAT HAVE YOU DONE WITH THE REAL G-MAN?

WHAT'S ALL THIS COMMOTION ABOUT?

IT'S *G-MAN*, PRINCIPAL JOHNSON! HE'S GOT A *NEW COSTUME!*

AND IT *SUCKS!*

ALL RIGHT, G-MAN...

...DO YOU HAVE A SIGNED *PERMISSION SLIP* FROM YOUR *PARENTS* TO WEAR THAT NEW COSTUME?

... NO.

THEN I'M GOING TO HAVE TO SEND YOU *HOME*, G-MAN. THAT'S *SCHOOL POLICY.* THERE'S NO TELLING *WHAT* THIS NEW COSTUME MEANS, OR *WHY* YOU'RE SUDDENLY *WEARING* IT. YOU'RE TOO BIG A RISK TO SCHOOL SAFETY WITH THAT STRANGE AND UNPREDICTABLE NEW OUTFIT. GO *HOME*, G-MAN... IF THAT'S WHO YOU REALLY *ARE.*

THAT COSTUME SUCKS!

WHAT ARE YOU DOING *BACK* ALREADY?

EVERYONE AT SCHOOL *FREAKED OUT* OVER THE NEW *COSTUME*, SO THEY SENT ME *HOME.* I TOLD YOU THIS WOULD *HAPPEN.*

WELL, I JUST FINISHED DOING THE *LAUNDRY.*

PUT ON YOUR REGULAR SUIT AND GO BACK TO SCHOOL.

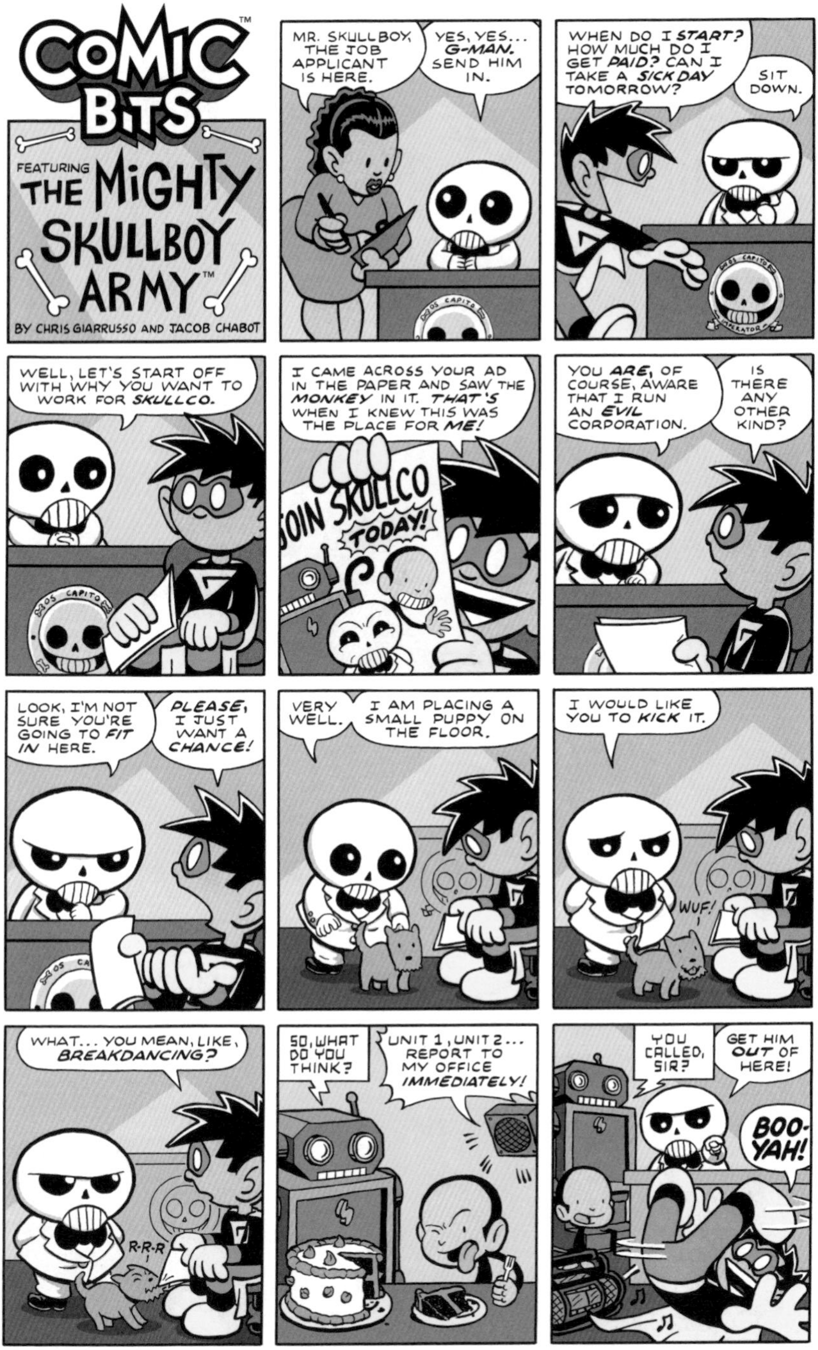
COMIC BITS™
FEATURING THE MIGHTY SKULLBOY ARMY™
BY CHRIS GIARRUSSO AND JACOB CHABOT
MR. SKULLBOY, THE JOB APPLICANT IS HERE.
YES, YES... G-MAN. SEND HIM IN.
WHEN DO I START? HOW MUCH DO I GET PAID? CAN I TAKE A SICK DAY TOMORROW?
SIT DOWN.
WELL, LET'S START OFF WITH WHY YOU WANT TO WORK FOR SKULLCO.
I CAME ACROSS YOUR AD IN THE PAPER AND SAW THE MONKEY IN IT. THAT'S WHEN I KNEW THIS WAS THE PLACE FOR ME!
JOIN SKULLCO TODAY!
YOU ARE, OF COURSE, AWARE THAT I RUN AN EVIL CORPORATION.
IS THERE ANY OTHER KIND?
LOOK, I'M NOT SURE YOU'RE GOING TO FIT IN HERE.
PLEASE, I JUST WANT A CHANCE!
VERY WELL.
I AM PLACING A SMALL PUPPY ON THE FLOOR.
I WOULD LIKE YOU TO KICK IT.
WUF!
WHAT... YOU MEAN, LIKE, BREAKDANCING?
R-R-R
SO, WHAT DO YOU THINK?
UNIT 1, UNIT 2... REPORT TO MY OFFICE IMMEDIATELY!
YOU CALLED, SIR?
GET HIM OUT OF HERE!
BOO-YAH!

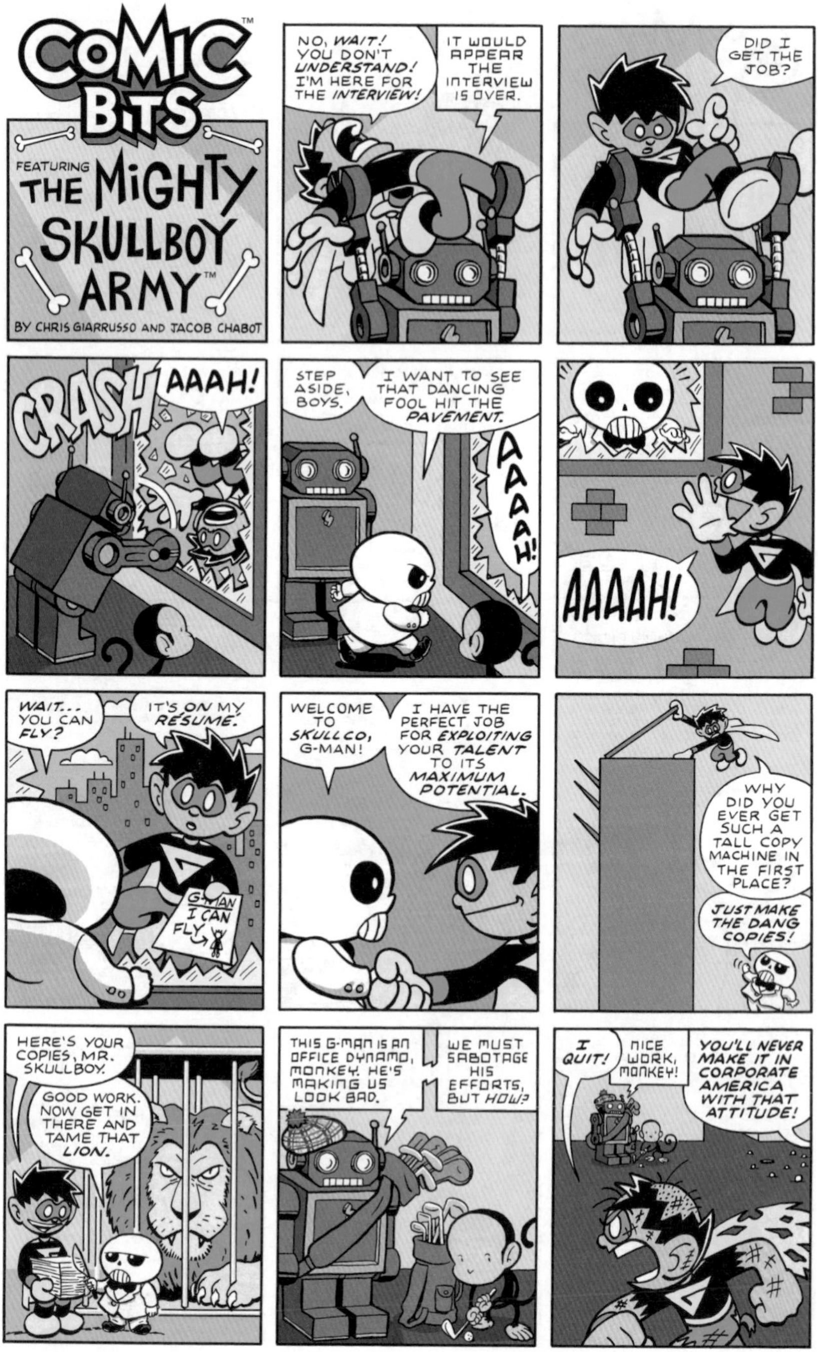
COMIC BITS™
FEATURING THE MIGHTY SKULLBOY ARMY™
BY CHRIS GIARRUSSO AND JACOB CHABOT
NO, WAIT! YOU DON'T UNDERSTAND! I'M HERE FOR THE INTERVIEW!
IT WOULD APPEAR THE INTERVIEW IS OVER.
DID I GET THE JOB?
CRASH
AAAH!
STEP ASIDE, BOYS.
I WANT TO SEE THAT DANCING FOOL HIT THE PAVEMENT.
AAAAAH!
AAAAH!
WAIT... YOU CAN FLY?
IT'S ON MY RÉSUMÉ.
G-MAN I CAN FLY
WELCOME TO SKULLCO, G-MAN!
I HAVE THE PERFECT JOB FOR EXPLOITING YOUR TALENT TO ITS MAXIMUM POTENTIAL.
WHY DID YOU EVER GET SUCH A TALL COPY MACHINE IN THE FIRST PLACE?
JUST MAKE THE DANG COPIES!
HERE'S YOUR COPIES, MR. SKULLBOY.
GOOD WORK. NOW GET IN THERE AND TAME THAT LION.
THIS G-MAN IS AN OFFICE DYNAMO, MONKEY. HE'S MAKING US LOOK BAD.
WE MUST SABOTAGE HIS EFFORTS, BUT HOW?
I QUIT!
NICE WORK, MONKEY!
YOU'LL NEVER MAKE IT IN CORPORATE AMERICA WITH THAT ATTITUDE!

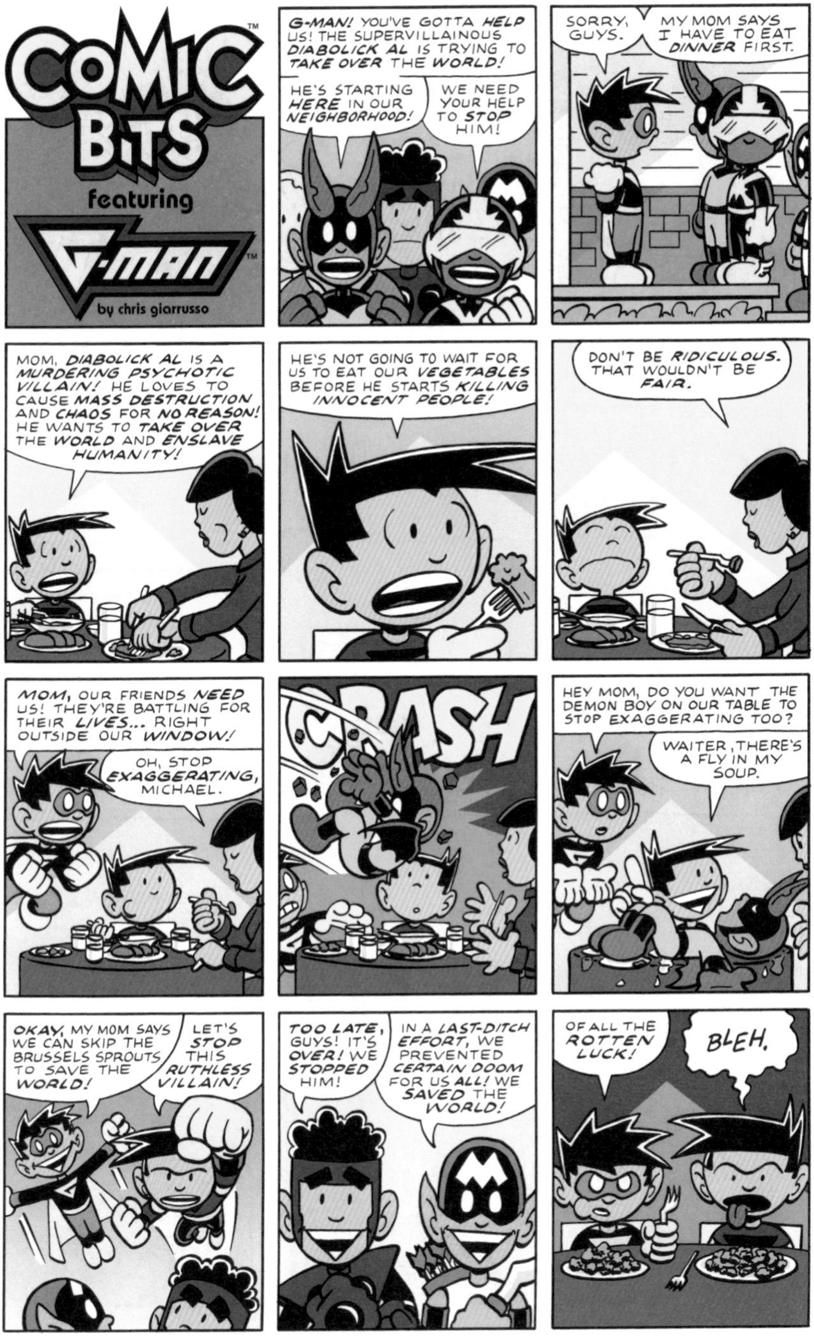
COMIC BITS™
featuring
G-MAN™
by chris giarrusso
G-MAN! YOU'VE GOTTA HELP US! THE SUPERVILLAINOUS DIABOLICK AL IS TRYING TO TAKE OVER THE WORLD!
HE'S STARTING HERE IN OUR NEIGHBORHOOD!
WE NEED YOUR HELP TO STOP HIM!
SORRY, GUYS.
MY MOM SAYS I HAVE TO EAT DINNER FIRST.
MOM, DIABOLICK AL IS A MURDERING PSYCHOTIC VILLAIN! HE LOVES TO CAUSE MASS DESTRUCTION AND CHAOS FOR NO REASON! HE WANTS TO TAKE OVER THE WORLD AND ENSLAVE HUMANITY!
HE'S NOT GOING TO WAIT FOR US TO EAT OUR VEGETABLES BEFORE HE STARTS KILLING INNOCENT PEOPLE!
DON'T BE RIDICULOUS. THAT WOULDN'T BE FAIR.
MOM, OUR FRIENDS NEED US! THEY'RE BATTLING FOR THEIR LIVES... RIGHT OUTSIDE OUR WINDOW!
OH, STOP EXAGGERATING, MICHAEL.
CRASH
HEY MOM, DO YOU WANT THE DEMON BOY ON OUR TABLE TO STOP EXAGGERATING TOO?
WAITER, THERE'S A FLY IN MY SOUP.
OKAY, MY MOM SAYS WE CAN SKIP THE BRUSSELS SPROUTS TO SAVE THE WORLD!
LET'S STOP THIS RUTHLESS VILLAIN!
TOO LATE, GUYS! IT'S OVER! WE STOPPED HIM!
IN A LAST-DITCH EFFORT, WE PREVENTED CERTAIN DOOM FOR US ALL! WE SAVED THE WORLD!
OF ALL THE ROTTEN LUCK!
BLEH.

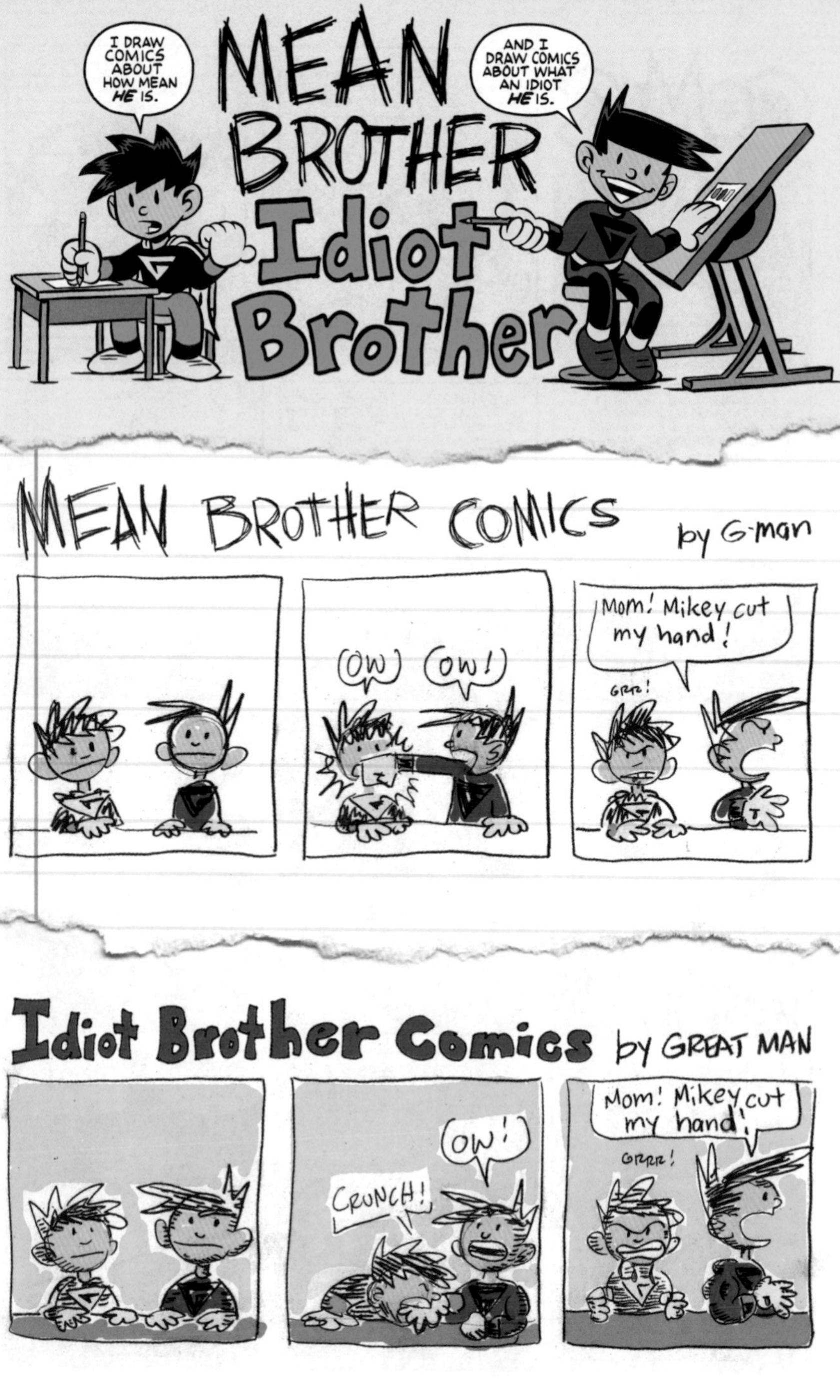

I DRAW COMICS ABOUT HOW MEAN HE IS.
MEAN BROTHER
AND I DRAW COMICS ABOUT WHAT AN IDIOT HE IS.
Idiot Brother
MEAN BROTHER COMICS
by G-man
OW
OW!
Mom! Mikey cut my hand!
GRR!
Idiot Brother Comics
by GREAT MAN
OW!
CRUNCH!
Mom! Mikey cut my hand!
GRRR!

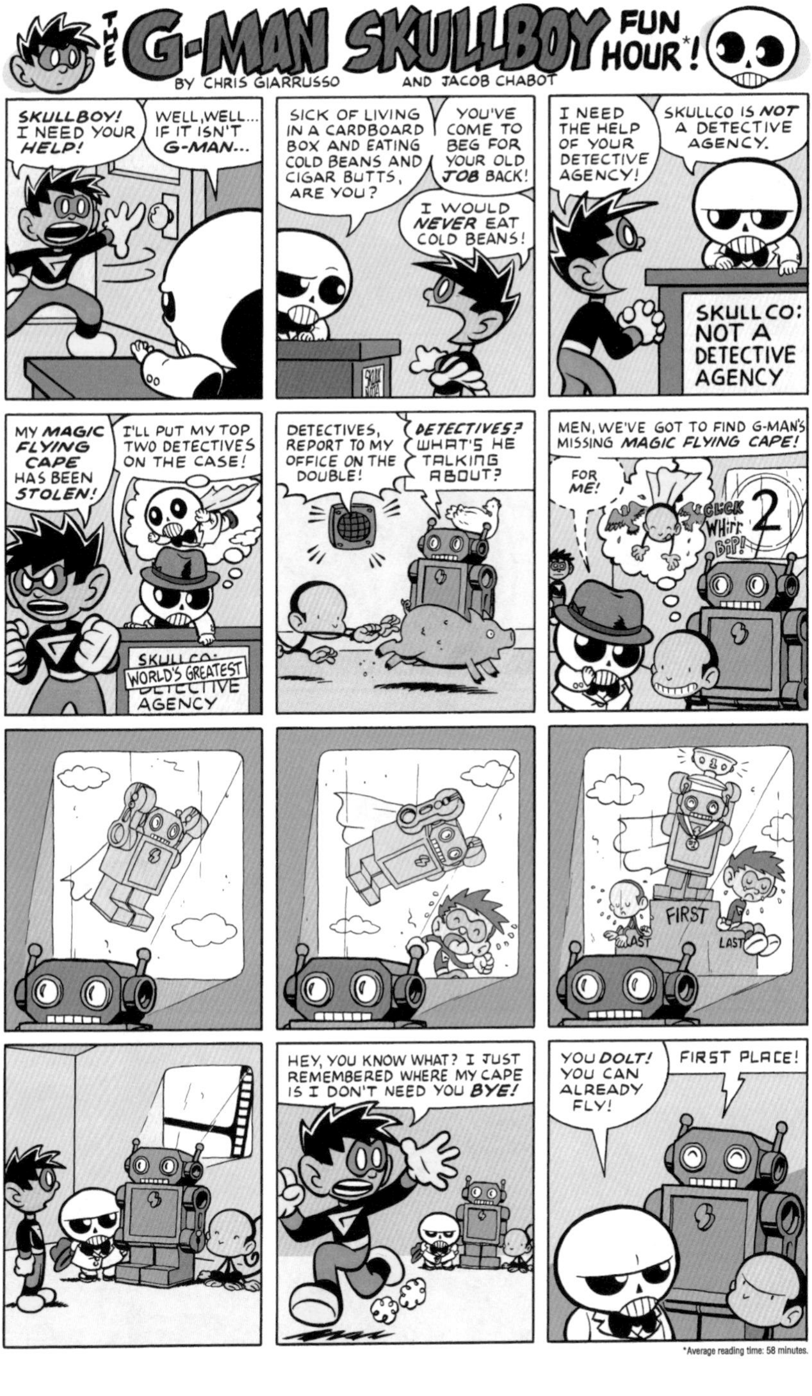
THE G-MAN SKULLBOY FUN HOUR*!
BY CHRIS GIARRUSSO AND JACOB CHABOT
SKULLBOY! I NEED YOUR HELP!
WELL, WELL... IF IT ISN'T G-MAN...
SICK OF LIVING IN A CARDBOARD BOX AND EATING COLD BEANS AND CIGAR BUTTS, ARE YOU?
YOU'VE COME TO BEG FOR YOUR OLD JOB BACK!
I WOULD NEVER EAT COLD BEANS!
I NEED THE HELP OF YOUR DETECTIVE AGENCY!
SKULLCO IS NOT A DETECTIVE AGENCY.
SKULLCO: NOT A DETECTIVE AGENCY
MY MAGIC FLYING CAPE HAS BEEN STOLEN!
I'LL PUT MY TOP TWO DETECTIVES ON THE CASE!
SKULLCO: WORLD'S GREATEST DETECTIVE AGENCY
DETECTIVES, REPORT TO MY OFFICE ON THE DOUBLE!
DETECTIVES? WHAT'S HE TALKING ABOUT?
MEN, WE'VE GOT TO FIND G-MAN'S MISSING MAGIC FLYING CAPE!
FOR ME!
CLICK
WHirr
BiP!
2
FIRST
LAST
LAST
HEY, YOU KNOW WHAT? I JUST REMEMBERED WHERE MY CAPE IS I DON'T NEED YOU BYE!
YOU DOLT! YOU CAN ALREADY FLY!
FIRST PLACE!

*Average reading time: 58 minutes.

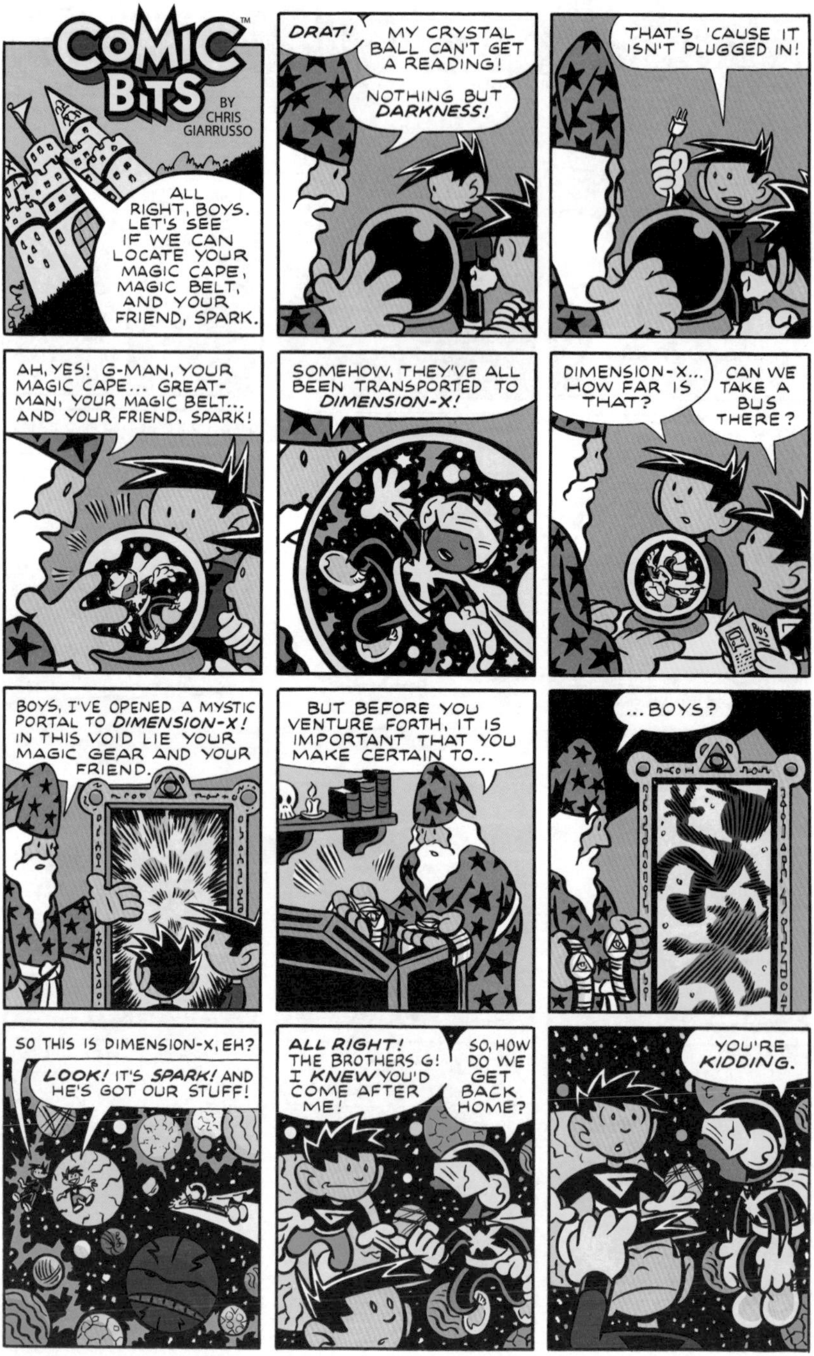
COMIC BITS™
BY CHRIS GIARRUSSO
ALL RIGHT, BOYS. LET'S SEE IF WE CAN LOCATE YOUR MAGIC CAPE, MAGIC BELT, AND YOUR FRIEND, SPARK.
DRAT!
MY CRYSTAL BALL CAN'T GET A READING!
NOTHING BUT DARKNESS!
THAT'S 'CAUSE IT ISN'T PLUGGED IN!
AH, YES! G-MAN, YOUR MAGIC CAPE... GREAT-MAN, YOUR MAGIC BELT... AND YOUR FRIEND, SPARK!
SOMEHOW, THEY'VE ALL BEEN TRANSPORTED TO DIMENSION-X!
DIMENSION-X... HOW FAR IS THAT?
CAN WE TAKE A BUS THERE?
BUS
BOYS, I'VE OPENED A MYSTIC PORTAL TO DIMENSION-X! IN THIS VOID LIE YOUR MAGIC GEAR AND YOUR FRIEND.
BUT BEFORE YOU VENTURE FORTH, IT IS IMPORTANT THAT YOU MAKE CERTAIN TO...
...BOYS?
SO THIS IS DIMENSION-X, EH?
LOOK! IT'S SPARK! AND HE'S GOT OUR STUFF!
ALL RIGHT! THE BROTHERS G! I KNEW YOU'D COME AFTER ME!
SO, HOW DO WE GET BACK HOME?
YOU'RE KIDDING.

SO, HOW ARE WE GOING TO GET BACK HOME?

I DON'T KNOW.

I'M STILL WONDERING WHY WE'RE HERE IN THE FIRST PLACE. WHAT OR WHO IS RESPONSIBLE FOR BRINGING US TO THIS *VOID?*

YOU! YOUR *MAGIC!*

GIVE ME YOUR *MAGIC!* I NEED YOUR *MAGIC!*

HEY, *STEP OFF*, PAL!

!

STEP OFF? I...YES, YOU'RE RIGHT.

MY *DESPERATION* HAS CAUSED ME TO FORGET MY *MANNERS.*

YOU SEE, A WAVE OF DARK MAGIC HAS INFECTED MY HOME WORLD AND THREATENS TO TEAR IT ASUNDER.

I USED A DIMENSIONAL TRANSPORTER TO LOCATE AND ACQUIRE ITEMS WITH SUFFICIENT MAGICAL POWER TO COMBAT THE DARK FORCES ENVELOPING MY WORLD...

...YOUR *CAPE...*

...YOUR *BELT...*

...AND YOUR *SHOES.*

PLEASE HELP ME BRING *SALVATION* TO MY *PEOPLE!*

HOW EVER CAN WE REFUSE SUCH A *NOBLE* REQUEST?

FOR T'WOULD BE AN ACT OF EVIL *ITSELF* WERE WE TO DENY.

SURE, JUST LEAD THE WAY, BUDDY.

THE DENIZENS OF MY HOME WORLD SHALL OWE YOU MANY THANKS! *THIS WAY!*

BOOM!

SO, HOW ARE WE GOING TO GET BACK HOME?

:SOB:

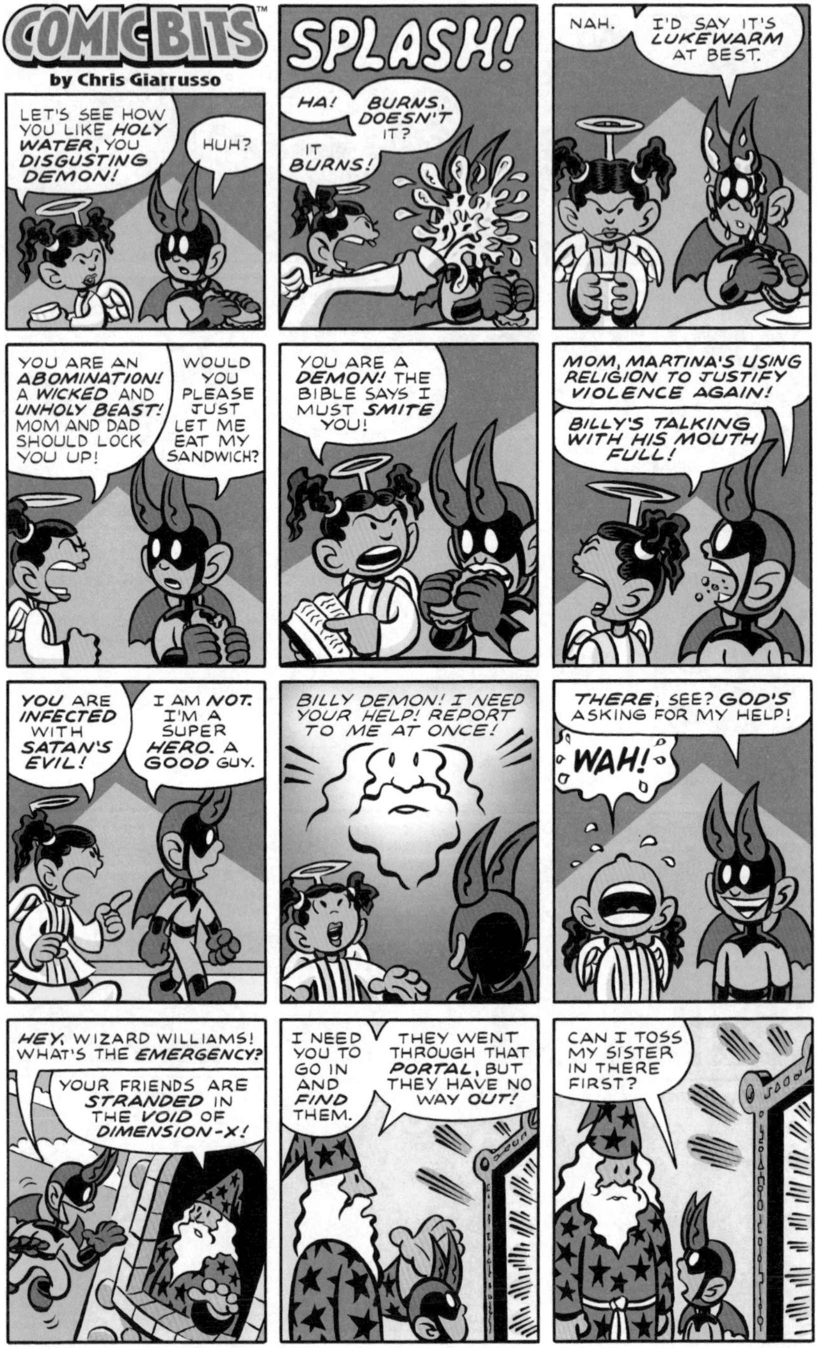
COMIC BITS™
by Chris Giarrusso
LET'S SEE HOW YOU LIKE HOLY WATER, YOU DISGUSTING DEMON!
HUH?
SPLASH!
HA!
IT BURNS!
BURNS, DOESN'T IT?
NAH.
I'D SAY IT'S LUKEWARM AT BEST.
YOU ARE AN ABOMINATION! A WICKED AND UNHOLY BEAST! MOM AND DAD SHOULD LOCK YOU UP!
WOULD YOU PLEASE JUST LET ME EAT MY SANDWICH?
YOU ARE A DEMON! THE BIBLE SAYS I MUST SMITE YOU!
MOM, MARTINA'S USING RELIGION TO JUSTIFY VIOLENCE AGAIN!
BILLY'S TALKING WITH HIS MOUTH FULL!
YOU ARE INFECTED WITH SATAN'S EVIL!
I AM NOT. I'M A SUPER HERO. A GOOD GUY.
BILLY DEMON! I NEED YOUR HELP! REPORT TO ME AT ONCE!
THERE, SEE? GOD'S ASKING FOR MY HELP!
WAH!
HEY, WIZARD WILLIAMS! WHAT'S THE EMERGENCY?
YOUR FRIENDS ARE STRANDED IN THE VOID OF DIMENSION-X!
I NEED YOU TO GO IN AND FIND THEM.
THEY WENT THROUGH THAT PORTAL, BUT THEY HAVE NO WAY OUT!
CAN I TOSS MY SISTER IN THERE FIRST?

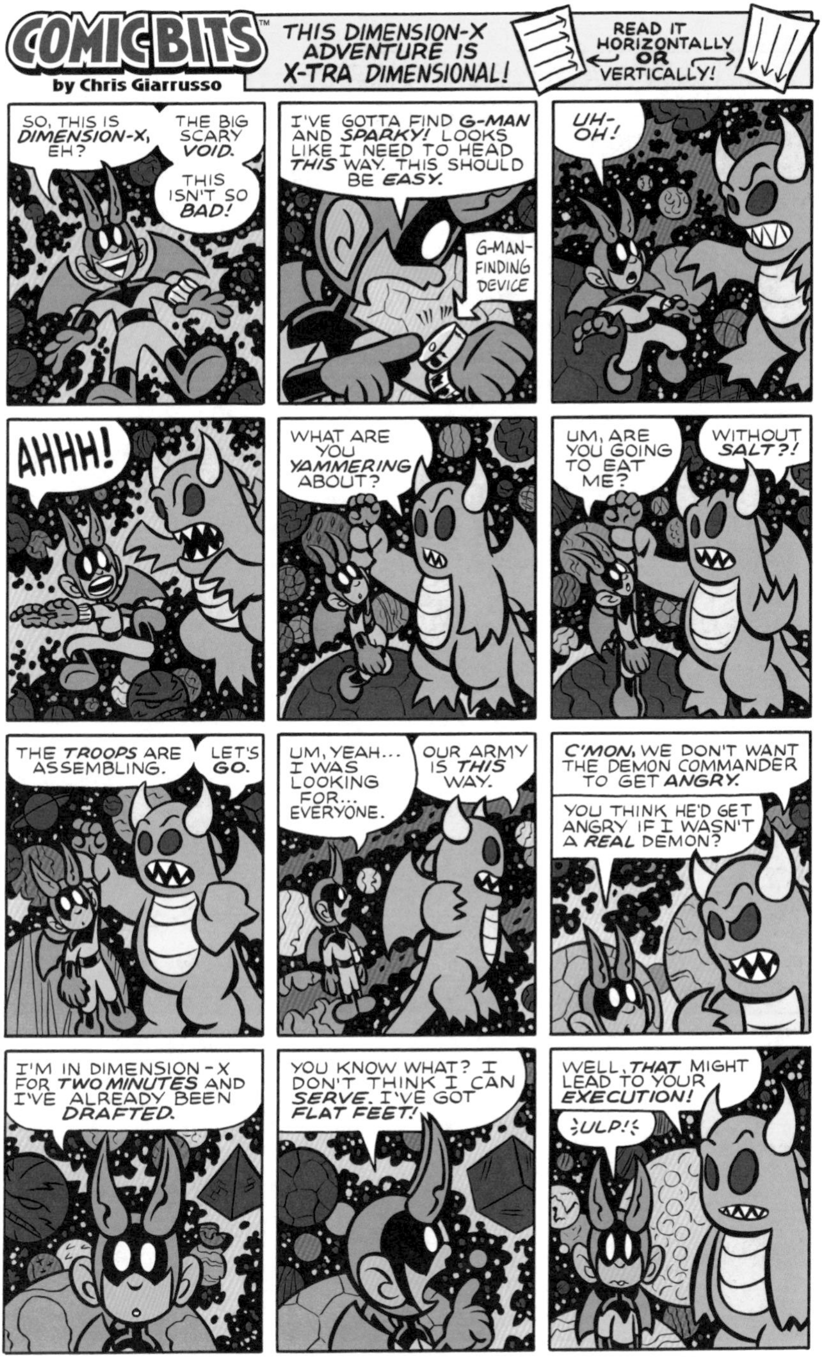
COMIC BITS™
by Chris Giarrusso
THIS DIMENSION-X ADVENTURE IS X-TRA DIMENSIONAL!
READ IT HORIZONTALLY OR VERTICALLY!
SO, THIS IS DIMENSION-X, EH?
THE BIG SCARY VOID.
THIS ISN'T SO BAD!
I'VE GOTTA FIND G-MAN AND SPARKY! LOOKS LIKE I NEED TO HEAD THIS WAY. THIS SHOULD BE EASY.
G-MAN-FINDING DEVICE
UH-OH!
AHHH!
WHAT ARE YOU YAMMERING ABOUT?
UM, ARE YOU GOING TO EAT ME?
WITHOUT SALT?!
THE TROOPS ARE ASSEMBLING.
LET'S GO.
UM, YEAH... I WAS LOOKING FOR... EVERYONE.
OUR ARMY IS THIS WAY.
C'MON, WE DON'T WANT THE DEMON COMMANDER TO GET ANGRY.
YOU THINK HE'D GET ANGRY IF I WASN'T A REAL DEMON?
I'M IN DIMENSION-X FOR TWO MINUTES AND I'VE ALREADY BEEN DRAFTED.
YOU KNOW WHAT? I DON'T THINK I CAN SERVE. I'VE GOT FLAT FEET!
WELL, THAT MIGHT LEAD TO YOUR EXECUTION!
ULP!

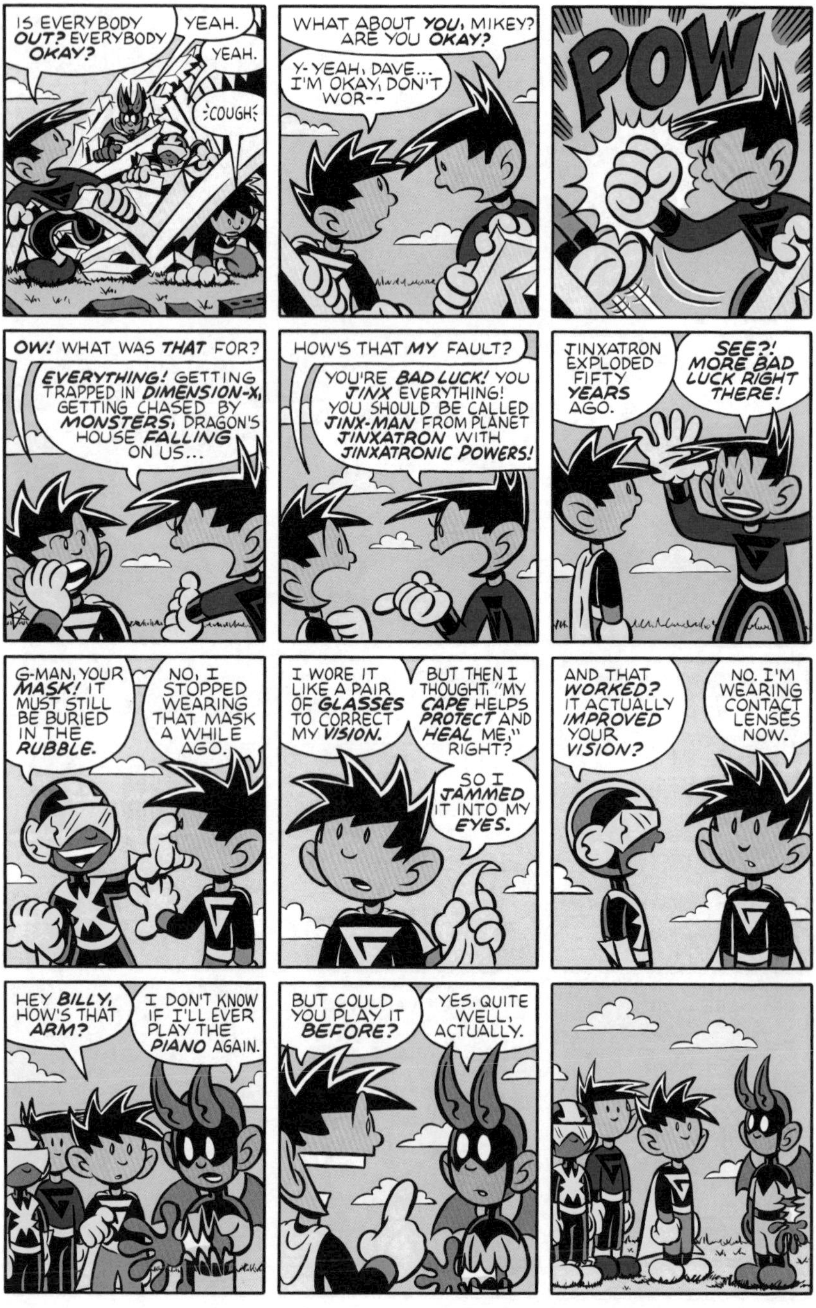

IS EVERYBODY OUT? EVERYBODY OKAY?
YEAH.
YEAH.
COUGH
WHAT ABOUT YOU, MIKEY? ARE YOU OKAY?
Y-YEAH, DAVE... I'M OKAY, DON'T WOR--
POW
OW! WHAT WAS THAT FOR?
EVERYTHING! GETTING TRAPPED IN DIMENSION-X, GETTING CHASED BY MONSTERS, DRAGON'S HOUSE FALLING ON US...
HOW'S THAT MY FAULT?
YOU'RE BAD LUCK! YOU JINX EVERYTHING! YOU SHOULD BE CALLED JINX-MAN FROM PLANET JINXATRON WITH JINXATRONIC POWERS!
JINXATRON EXPLODED FIFTY YEARS AGO.
SEE?! MORE BAD LUCK RIGHT THERE!
G-MAN, YOUR MASK! IT MUST STILL BE BURIED IN THE RUBBLE.
NO, I STOPPED WEARING THAT MASK A WHILE AGO.
I WORE IT LIKE A PAIR OF GLASSES TO CORRECT MY VISION.
BUT THEN I THOUGHT, "MY CAPE HELPS PROTECT AND HEAL ME," RIGHT?
SO I JAMMED IT INTO MY EYES.
AND THAT WORKED? IT ACTUALLY IMPROVED YOUR VISION?
NO. I'M WEARING CONTACT LENSES NOW.
HEY BILLY, HOW'S THAT ARM?
I DON'T KNOW IF I'LL EVER PLAY THE PIANO AGAIN.
BUT COULD YOU PLAY IT BEFORE?
YES, QUITE WELL, ACTUALLY.

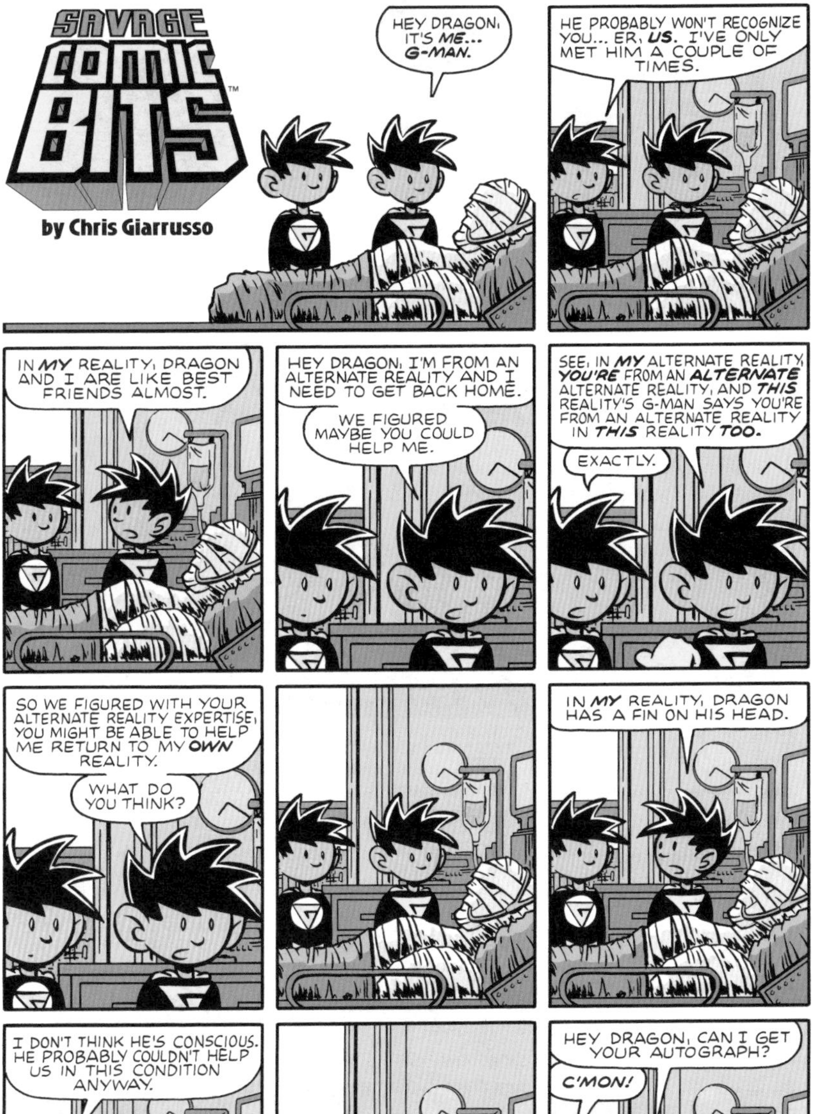
SAVAGE COMIC BITS™
by Chris Giarrusso
HEY DRAGON, IT'S ME... G-MAN.
HE PROBABLY WON'T RECOGNIZE YOU... ER, US. I'VE ONLY MET HIM A COUPLE OF TIMES.
IN MY REALITY, DRAGON AND I ARE LIKE BEST FRIENDS ALMOST.
HEY DRAGON, I'M FROM AN ALTERNATE REALITY AND I NEED TO GET BACK HOME.
WE FIGURED MAYBE YOU COULD HELP ME.
SEE, IN MY ALTERNATE REALITY, YOU'RE FROM AN ALTERNATE ALTERNATE REALITY, AND THIS REALITY'S G-MAN SAYS YOU'RE FROM AN ALTERNATE REALITY IN THIS REALITY TOO.
EXACTLY.
SO WE FIGURED WITH YOUR ALTERNATE REALITY EXPERTISE, YOU MIGHT BE ABLE TO HELP ME RETURN TO MY OWN REALITY.
WHAT DO YOU THINK?
IN MY REALITY, DRAGON HAS A FIN ON HIS HEAD.
I DON'T THINK HE'S CONSCIOUS. HE PROBABLY COULDN'T HELP US IN THIS CONDITION ANYWAY.
HEY DRAGON, CAN I GET YOUR AUTOGRAPH?
C'MON!

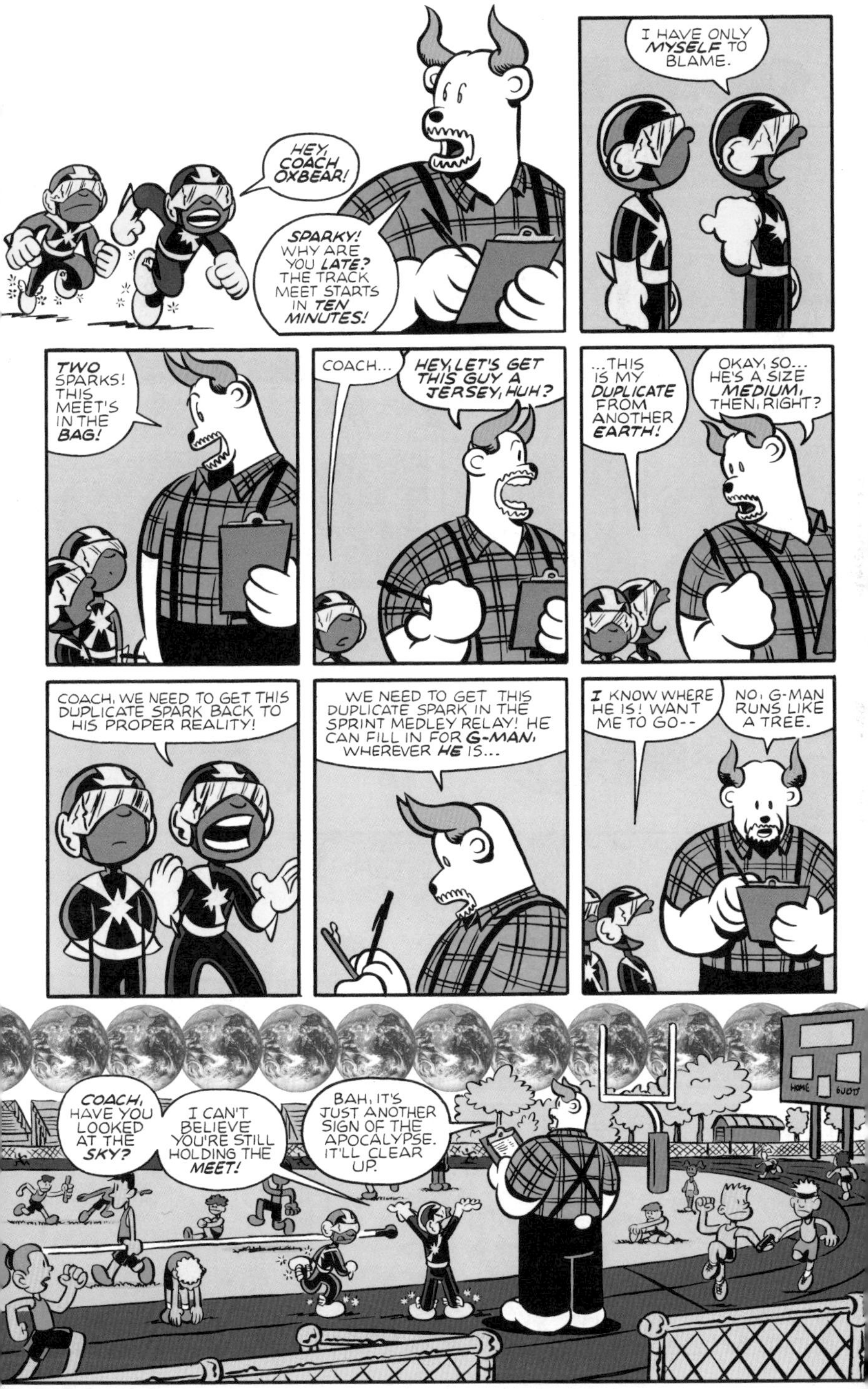
HEY, COACH OXBEAR!
SPARKY! WHY ARE YOU LATE? THE TRACK MEET STARTS IN TEN MINUTES!
I HAVE ONLY MYSELF TO BLAME.
TWO SPARKS! THIS MEET'S IN THE BAG!
COACH...
HEY, LET'S GET THIS GUY A JERSEY, HUH?
...THIS IS MY DUPLICATE FROM ANOTHER EARTH!
OKAY, SO... HE'S A SIZE MEDIUM, THEN, RIGHT?
COACH, WE NEED TO GET THIS DUPLICATE SPARK BACK TO HIS PROPER REALITY!
WE NEED TO GET THIS DUPLICATE SPARK IN THE SPRINT MEDLEY RELAY! HE CAN FILL IN FOR G-MAN, WHEREVER HE IS...
I KNOW WHERE HE IS! WANT ME TO GO--
NO, G-MAN RUNS LIKE A TREE.
COACH, HAVE YOU LOOKED AT THE SKY?
I CAN'T BELIEVE YOU'RE STILL HOLDING THE MEET!
BAH, IT'S JUST ANOTHER SIGN OF THE APOCALYPSE. IT'LL CLEAR UP.
HOME
GUEST

Wrote by Chris Giarrusso & Jacob Chabot   Drawed by Jacob Chabot

Comic Bits and THE MIGHTY SKULLBOY ARMY

Wrote by Chris Giarrusso & Jacob Chabot
Drawn by Chris Giarrusso

AWW! LOOK AT THAT. HE'S ALL TUCKERED OUT.

IT'S BEEN A LONG DAY, MEN. GET SOME REST. I'M GOING TO PUT A FEW MORE HOURS IN.

♫ ROCK-A-BYE MONKEY...♫

SKULLBOY! WE GOTTA *TALK* TO YOU, CHUMP!

I'M SORRY, MR. SKULLBOY. THEY JUST BARGED RIGHT IN!

?

HEY! YOU'RE AN ALTERNATE REALITY *G-MAN!* WHAT'S WITH THE EYEPATCH?

WHATTAYA *THINK*, BONEHEAD?!

YEAH. DON'T THEY HAVE MANNERS WHERE YOU'RE FROM?

NEVER MIND *THAT!* LOOK OUT THE WINDOW!

OH YES, THE ALTERNATE REALITY CRISIS. PERHAPS *TOGETHER* WE CAN RESTORE *BALANCE* AND--

BALANCE, *SHMALANCE!* GO TALK TA *JACK PALANCE!*

WE'RE GONNA BLOW THEM OTHER EARTHS OUTTA THE *SKY!*

WHEN WE'RE THE ONLY PLANET LEFT, *WE'LL* CONTROL THE WHOLE *UNIVERSE!* WE JUST NEED YOUR HELP TO...

BUT... BUT I JUST RUN A SMALL NON-PROFIT ORGANIZATION! I COULDN'T HELP YOU EVEN IF I *WANTED* TO! YOU GUYS ARE *INSANE!*

QUIT FLAPPIN' YER *MANGDIBULA!* WE KNOW YER *ROBOT'S* PACKIN' *MAJOR FIREPOWER!*

THE KID'S GOT A CANNON FER AN ARM, I TELL YA'! A *CANNON!*

NO! I CAN'T LET YOU USE MY RESOURCES FOR *EVIL!*

YOU GOT NO *CHOICE!* IT'S *THEM* OR *US!* YOU DON'T THINK *THEY'RE* SCHEMIN' TO GET US *FIRST?!* WE GOTTA BEAT 'EM TO THE *PUNCH*, SEE?

WHICH ARM IS IT?

ONLY ONE WAY TO FIND OUT! MAKE A *WISH!*

GENTLEMEN, I DO PROTEST...

MINE! *I WIN!*

HEY... WHAT'S THAT IN THE SK--

BOOM

WHAT'D YOU WISH FOR?

IF *I TELL* YOU, IT WON'T COME *TRUE.*

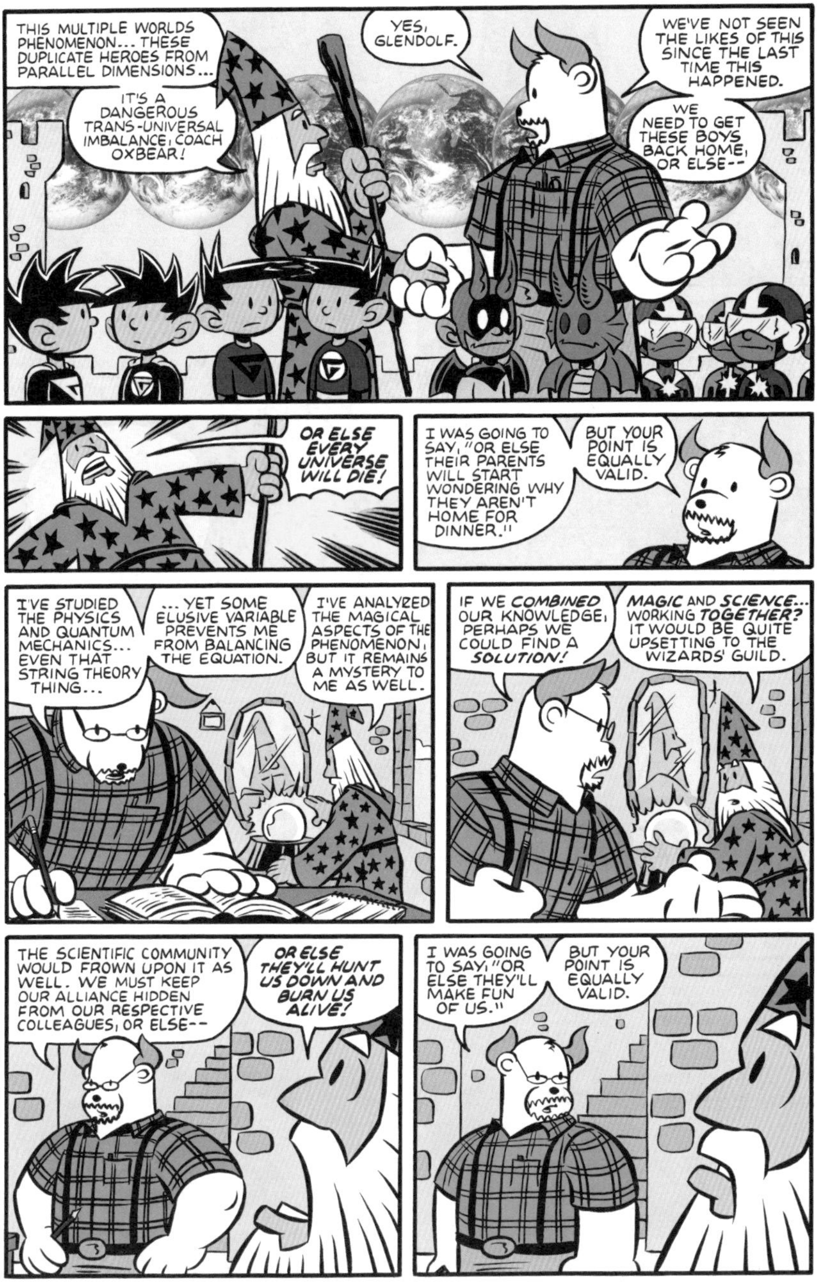
THIS MULTIPLE WORLDS PHENOMENON... THESE DUPLICATE HEROES FROM PARALLEL DIMENSIONS...
IT'S A DANGEROUS TRANS-UNIVERSAL IMBALANCE, COACH OXBEAR!
YES, GLENDOLF.
WE'VE NOT SEEN THE LIKES OF THIS SINCE THE LAST TIME THIS HAPPENED.
WE NEED TO GET THESE BOYS BACK HOME, OR ELSE--
OR ELSE EVERY UNIVERSE WILL DIE!
I WAS GOING TO SAY, "OR ELSE THEIR PARENTS WILL START WONDERING WHY THEY AREN'T HOME FOR DINNER."
BUT YOUR POINT IS EQUALLY VALID.
I'VE STUDIED THE PHYSICS AND QUANTUM MECHANICS... EVEN THAT STRING THEORY THING...
...YET SOME ELUSIVE VARIABLE PREVENTS ME FROM BALANCING THE EQUATION.
I'VE ANALYZED THE MAGICAL ASPECTS OF THE PHENOMENON, BUT IT REMAINS A MYSTERY TO ME AS WELL.
IF WE COMBINED OUR KNOWLEDGE, PERHAPS WE COULD FIND A SOLUTION!
MAGIC AND SCIENCE... WORKING TOGETHER? IT WOULD BE QUITE UPSETTING TO THE WIZARDS' GUILD.
THE SCIENTIFIC COMMUNITY WOULD FROWN UPON IT AS WELL. WE MUST KEEP OUR ALLIANCE HIDDEN FROM OUR RESPECTIVE COLLEAGUES, OR ELSE--
OR ELSE THEY'LL HUNT US DOWN AND BURN US ALIVE!
I WAS GOING TO SAY, "OR ELSE THEY'LL MAKE FUN OF US."
BUT YOUR POINT IS EQUALLY VALID.

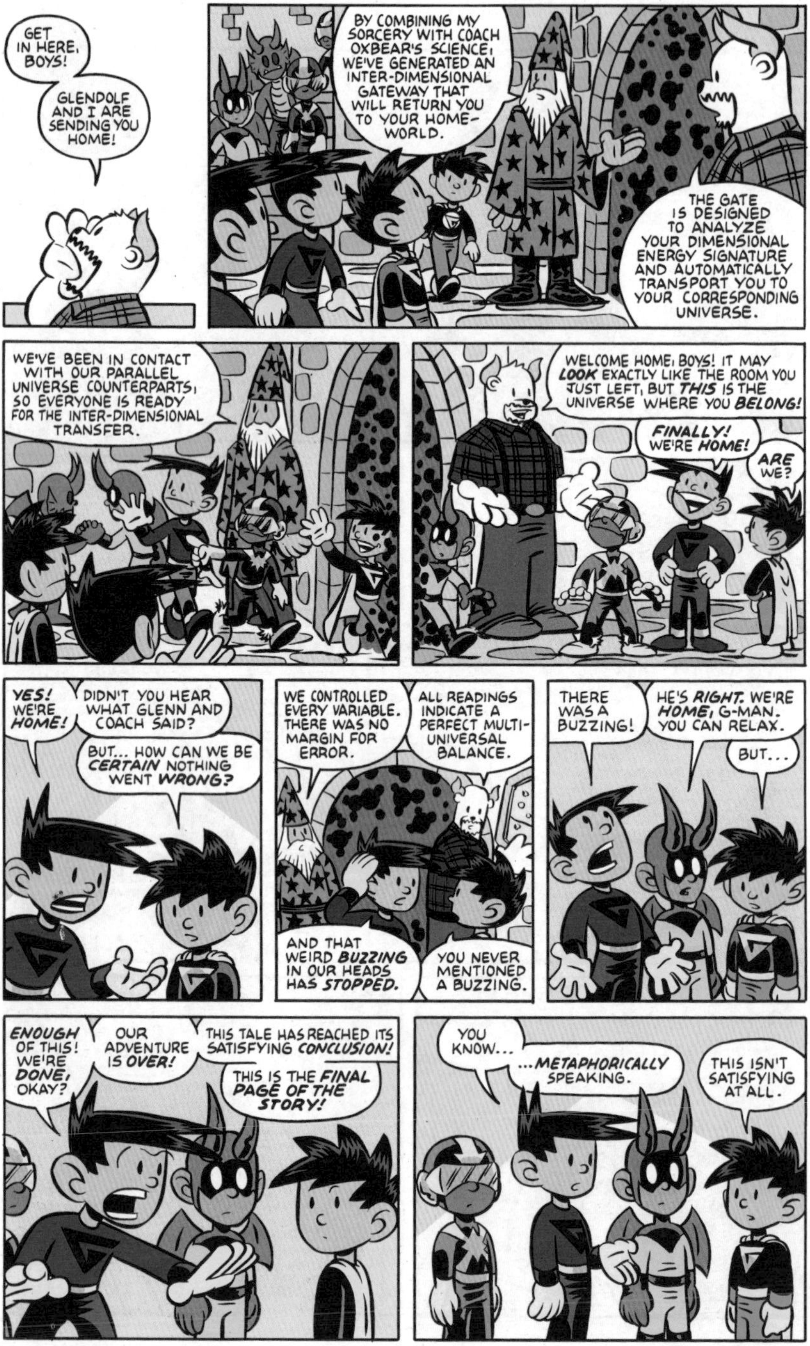
GET IN HERE, BOYS!
GLENDOLF AND I ARE SENDING YOU HOME!
BY COMBINING MY SORCERY WITH COACH OXBEAR'S SCIENCE, WE'VE GENERATED AN INTER-DIMENSIONAL GATEWAY THAT WILL RETURN YOU TO YOUR HOME-WORLD.
THE GATE IS DESIGNED TO ANALYZE YOUR DIMENSIONAL ENERGY SIGNATURE AND AUTOMATICALLY TRANSPORT YOU TO YOUR CORRESPONDING UNIVERSE.
WE'VE BEEN IN CONTACT WITH OUR PARALLEL UNIVERSE COUNTERPARTS, SO EVERYONE IS READY FOR THE INTER-DIMENSIONAL TRANSFER.
WELCOME HOME, BOYS! IT MAY LOOK EXACTLY LIKE THE ROOM YOU JUST LEFT, BUT THIS IS THE UNIVERSE WHERE YOU BELONG!
FINALLY! WE'RE HOME!
ARE WE?
YES! WE'RE HOME!
DIDN'T YOU HEAR WHAT GLENN AND COACH SAID?
BUT... HOW CAN WE BE CERTAIN NOTHING WENT WRONG?
WE CONTROLLED EVERY VARIABLE. THERE WAS NO MARGIN FOR ERROR.
ALL READINGS INDICATE A PERFECT MULTI-UNIVERSAL BALANCE.
AND THAT WEIRD BUZZING IN OUR HEADS HAS STOPPED.
YOU NEVER MENTIONED A BUZZING.
THERE WAS A BUZZING!
HE'S RIGHT. WE'RE HOME, G-MAN. YOU CAN RELAX.
BUT...
ENOUGH OF THIS! WE'RE DONE, OKAY?
OUR ADVENTURE IS OVER!
THIS TALE HAS REACHED ITS SATISFYING CONCLUSION!
THIS IS THE FINAL PAGE OF THE STORY!
YOU KNOW...
...METAPHORICALLY SPEAKING.
THIS ISN'T SATISFYING AT ALL.

THE END